Why Shoot the Teacher

Why Shoot the Teacher

Max Braithwaite

McClelland and Stewart Limited

Reprinted 1975, 1976

The Canadian Publishers
McClelland and Stewart Limited
25 Hollinger Road, Toronto

ISBN 0-7710-1599-2

PRINTED AND BOUND IN CANADA

To MAC *who was there too*

Contents

Why Shoot the Teacher

1 un or freeze

At twenty-five minutes after two on the afternoon of the third of January, 1933, I stepped out of a frost-covered C.N.R. passenger car onto the worn, wooden platform of Bleke, Saskatchewan. Since then, when I've permitted myself to think of it at all, I've been convinced it was then and there that I began to lose my mind.

The train that fetched me was what they call a "mixed". This means it was made up of freight cars carrying articles of some value such as farm machinery, rock salt, pigs, or gopher traps, and one passenger car tacked like an afterthought on the tail end, carrying what seemed to have no value on the prairies then – people.

To be accurate, since leaving the town of Mantario where the clergyman I'd been talking to got off, the car had carried only me. This was my first real experience with loneliness, the most desperate and deadly of all conditions. For the whole of my stay in this desolate district I was to fight against it with every stratagem I could devise, and I was to lose.

A couple of frost-bearded trainmen, with earlugs tied

under their chins and gauntlet mitts on their hands, tipped my heavy trunk out the door of the baggage car and wrestled it onto the platform. They slanted perfunctory glances my way, perhaps wondering if, from its weight, it might contain a dead body. Actually it contained the only thing worth more than twenty dollars I owned in the world, a brand new, never-opened ten-volume encyclopaedia.

In point of actual fact, I didn't even own those books. I'd stolen them before leaving home. But that's another story.

Having also unloaded a carton of canned goods, a half dozen empty cream cans, and a small sack containing a part for a harness, the men pushed the door shut. The "mixed" puffed off down the track, and with it went just about every vestige of the twentieth century I was to see for a while. For, although I didn't realize it then, I had stepped out of the world of electricity, automobiles, radios, and well-marked streets into a world where few of these existed and where nature's old law of be tough or perish was still very much in vogue.

Pulling my face down behind my thin overcoat collar, I looked around the settlement. It consisted of two grain elevators, a coal shed, a ramshackle building that served as a store, one frame house banked high with snow, and nothing more. A tiny oasis of futility on a barren sea of despair.

The storm door of the store opened; the wind caught it and banged it back. A big man buried in a ragged buffalo-hide overcoat and with a scarf tied around his neck and over his head advanced across the road towards me. With a shock I noticed that around his feet, in lieu of overshoes, he had wound ordinary gunny sacks, two for each foot.

"You the teacher?" he mumbled when he came within earshot. Nothing more. No pleasant introduction, no smile of welcome, no hearty handshake. He obviously resented me on sight, and somehow I'd expected him to. For one of the peculiarities of the depression on the prairies, and one

I've never had satisfactorily explained, was the way that older people resented the young. It was as though they blamed them for the drought and poor prices and the death of their hopes. Probably not. More likely the long series of hopeless years culminating in these near-starvation conditions, made them mad at everything, including a city boy standing alone on a bare platform wondering how he'd got there and why.

"Name's McDougall," the big man mumbled. "Secretary of Willowgreen School District." His small, wind-worn eyes scanned me from head to foot before he added, as though realizing belatedly that even an idiot was entitled to some kind of warning, "It's a twelve-mile drive out to the district."

A twelve-mile drive. Although I'd been born and had spent my entire twenty years in Saskatchewan, I still didn't fully understand the terrible meaning of those words. For I had lived most of my life in the city of Saskatoon, and life in a Saskatchewan city is little different from that of a city anywhere. Oh, the weather gets colder – an average January temperature of minus 1 degrees – that's true. But the houses are well insulated and warm, streetcars comfortable enough, automobiles well equipped with heaters. Young people dress much the same as their counterparts in Toronto or New York: light overcoats, lined leather gloves. On my feet I had one pair of socks and a pair of oxfords with toe rubbers. I had never been in rural Saskatchewan in the winter in my life. I didn't know that the words "twelve-mile drive" were the equivalent of "trial by frost-bite".

Without another word Dave McDougall bent over and took hold of the leather handle at one end of my roped-up trunk. I took the other. He inclined his cloth-swathed head towards the end of the platform where a team of lean, shaggy Clydes stood, heads low against the wind. We staggered to the sleigh and slid the trunk over the side onto the thin layer of straw in the bottom. McDougall hunched himself down into the bottom of the two-deck sleigh box and pulled his buffalo coat tight around his knees. Then he clucked to the team. Demonstrating some sort of city-wise flamboyance that I suppose I thought necessary, I perched myself on top of the trunk exposed to the biting wind and snow.

The team wheeled slowly and plodded along the one short street. A black and white farm collie with fur like that of a winter wolf made a few jumps at the noses of the team and then began ranging after rabbits.

There was no straight road. In those days highways and township roads weren't ploughed clean of snow in winter. Rather they were abandoned entirely, and the first farmer to come along with a sleigh established a trail that followed the line of least resistance across the fields, winding around hills, snow drifts and brier patches. Those farmers who were lucky enough still to be driving cars simply put them up on wooden blocks for the winter and took to cutter and sleigh.

It was some trip. Twelve miles with a team undernourished on wheat straw takes at least three hours. The temperature was somewhere below minus thirty degrees Fahrenheit, and there was the usual persistent, biting wind out of the northwest, a wind that was getting stronger. It soon became perfectly clear to me that I had two choices: I could either sit in the sleigh box and freeze, or I could get out and run behind.

I ran behind.

And while this twenty-year-old, filled with restless vitality, arrogance, and frustration, plods along behind that sleigh box, puffing his breath against a skimpy collar to salvage some of its warmth, trying to keep his ears, cheeks, and nose covered with thinly gloved hands, let's consider where he is and how he comes to be there.

This is the semi-arid region that lies on the Saskatchewan-Alberta border just north of the South Saskatchewan

River. Although it lies next door to the flat, heavy-soiled wheatland of the Kindersley plain, it bears no resemblance to it. This slightly rolling, treeless, curly-grass country should never have been broken up for farmland. No prosperous farmsteads with large, white L-shaped houses and big red barns are seen from the road. Rather the flat-roofed, unpainted barns and shack-like houses. And everywhere Russian thistle poking spiny twigs through the snow.

The people who lived here were the usual pioneers from Ontario, the United States, Britain, and central Europe. They had come, filled with hope and vigour, to the "Golden West" to make a home and a future. They remained in a gritty dustbowl, their souls scarred by a smouldering resentment and a keen sense of betrayal. They stayed on for the least attractive of all reasons – because they couldn't get out. In those days before family allowances there was often no cash money in a house for months at a time. This accounted for the gunny sacks on Dave McDougall's feet. He literally didn't have the $3.98 to send to Eaton's for a pair of overshoes.

I didn't know all this as I stumbled along behind that sleigh box. Times were hard, I knew. They had been hard in Saskatoon ever since the stock-market crash of 1929 had officially opened "the great depression", and made it impossible for me to attend University. In fact, I'd had to borrow money to finish Normal School.

That was the first big resentment. I'd never wanted to go to Normal School. Then, as now, the better students in high school looked upon elementary-school teaching as a second-rate occupation, useful at best as a way to pick up a quick thousand dollars so that you might continue your education.

So, until prosperity would come bursting around that corner where President Hoover had said it was lurking, I went to the Saskatoon Normal School. Since I didn't want to be there, I contributed little to that institution and learned nothing about teaching.

How do you teach a person to teach, anyway? A medical student can be instructed in where the vital parts of the body are located, and how to remove and replace them. A dentist practises with drill and chisel. But teaching, it has always seemed to me, is something that must be learned by trial and error and by the development of a subtle feel for it, like flying an aircraft by the seat of your pants. To be sure we learned about the theories of education (Dewey's progressive ideas were beginning to influence educationalists) and the methods of some great teachers of the past. We made charts and time-tables and books of nursery rhymes and spent a confusing two weeks in urban and rural schools as "normalites". Then we were released on the unsuspecting youth of the province.

But nobody wanted us. During the ten months at Normal School the teaching profession had degenerated frightfully. Now there were hundreds of applicants for every job. After carefully clipping the "Teachers Wanted" ads from the paper, I began writing applications in my best handwriting and according to the rules laid down by our English instructor. At first I was choosy, selecting only schools close to the city and in reasonably sized towns. My original asking price was $1,000 per annum, considered a good price for teachers in those days, and corresponding now to an annual salary in the neighbourhood of $4,000.

There were no takers.

After twenty-five letters I became less selective as to location and size of school and dropped my price to $800. Still not a nibble.

From there my preference diminished until I was offering to teach anywhere for whatever they'd pay. I wrote by actual count over a hundred applications, but not one single reply did I get.

Then I took to visiting school boards, borrowing my brother's car or badgering a cousin into driving me. During the hot, dusty evenings of August I interviewed school boards in front of hardware stores, in the offices of lumber yards, and in grain elevators. I trudged for miles over stubble fields to extol my credentials to tired farmers sitting impatiently on binders or manure spreaders. I swore I neither smoked, nor drank, nor went out with girls (all lies). Depending on whom I was talking to I was United Church, Baptist, Presbyterian, or Anglican. I'd have been Hindu if that would have helped. I promised to teach Sunday School, lead the Boy Scouts, coach softball, board with the chairman, play catch for the baseball team, and start an athletic club for older boys.

They yawned in my face.

When people talk of jobs being scarce now, I just don't know what they mean. That was real unemployment. Of the 200 students who attended the Normal School that year only a handful got jobs. Many never taught at all. University graduates fared little better. It was said – and I can believe it – that of the entire graduating class of engineers that year one man got a job. And that was a job driving a truck.

The desperation for jobs passes belief. Occupations such as being a fireman, delivering milk or bread, clerking in the Hudson's Bay Store, had a very high priority, because they were steady. They told a joke in Saskatoon about the man who fell into the Saskatchewan River and five men, leaning over the bridge, shouted questions to him concerning his name and place of employment. On learning this, they raced off in an attempt to get his job, leaving the poor fellow to drown.

I never laughed at that joke. It was too close to grim truth for humour.

As the fall wore on and advertisements for teachers disappeared, I resigned myself to being unemployed. I helped my mother with the weekly wash, waxed acres of floors, feuded with an older working brother about whether "non-paying boarders" had any bathroom rights, bought Turret cigarettes one at a time at the drugstore, and slowly degenerated.

Then, one day after Christmas, to pass the time, I went to a hockey game involving the newly built technical school, and decided to enroll in that institution. Since there was no thought of getting a job anyway, I selected a trade that I thought might be helpful one day – motor mechanics. I attended one class and learned how to solder a radiator. Then, when I'd given up the idea of ever teaching, the letter came from McDougall offering me the job at Willowgreen School.

So, I quit technical school, and the world lost a fumbling motor mechanic. I wrote McDougall that I would accept the job, although I knew nothing about the conditions there, and he replied, advising me to be at Bleke on the third of January.

I had no money and no decent clothing. For train fare I went to a former Sunday School teacher and hockey coach and begged a loan. From the attic Mother resurrected an old steamer trunk that had a warped wooden tray covered with flowered paper and smelled of mothballs. Into this I packed my meagre belongings and looked around for something else with which to fill it.

On the front porch of our house on Tenth Street sat an unopened cardboard carton containing ten volumes of an educational encyclopaedia. The manner of its being there was typical of Saskatchewan in the early thirties. The lack of regular jobs had forced many aggressive young men into the business of selling insurance, magazine subscriptions, and sets of books. Their favourite targets were the teachers in one-room rural schools who had a little cash and were usually so lonely they would talk to anyone.

My sister was one of these. The encyclopaedia salesman dropped in during morning classes when she was trying to keep eight grades busy at once. He insisted on giving his sales pitch, and, to get rid of him, she signed the piece of paper he placed in front of her. Then, after he left, she read it and discovered she had contracted to pay $159.98 for a set of the books. Since this was one third of her yearly salary, she immediately wrote to the company to cancel the order. They wrote a crisp letter on crisp paper saying that a deal was a deal and the books would be delivered.

They were delivered. But my sister, who had her own way of dealing with such contingencies, simply refused to remove them from the verandah. There they sat. The company wouldn't take them back; my sister wouldn't take them in. I noticed them when I was packing my sparse belongings and dumped them into my trunk. When the company billed my sister for the books, she could truthfully say she didn't have them. When they billed me, I ignored them, secure in the knowledge that no one would follow me to Bleke, Saskatchewan.

And so, with my trunk and books riding, I walked or trotted most of the twelve miles from Bleke station to Willowgreen School District. Now and then, when I was taking a breather, Dave McDougall would mumble a question at me. But mostly he just sat with his broad rump against the side of the sleigh box and his knees pulled up in front of him, so that everything was covered by the buffalo coat. He didn't need to glance sideways at the team. They knew the trail and followed it home.

I didn't actually get frost-bitten during that drive, but merely did the kind of "freezing" I had been doing all my life. That is, my ear lobes became stiff and white and, when I rubbed them, red and sore. The same with my nose, fingers, and toes.

It was pitch dark when we reached the collection of

shacks that made up the McDougall homestead. All I could see as we approached over the flat field was a dim yellow glow flickering through a patched windowpane. When McDougall pulled up to the door, I noticed that the unpainted frame house was banked to the window sills with manure.

"You go on in," he said. "I'll unhitch. No use in taking your trunk out of the sleigh until we figure out where you're going to live."

He shouted "Ha-low!" and the door was shoved open by a short, shapeless woman in a worn dress and long cardigan sweater. Behind her crowded four small children. I entered a small square room that was dominated by an enormous kitchen range and cluttered with outdoor clothing and a set of harness somebody had been mending. A shaggy farm collie got stiffly to its feet from behind the stove and growled a welcome. Mrs. McDougall held out a worn, rough hand, and muttered a greeting. Then, pushing the children forward, she said, "These here are some of your class, Teacher. Mary and Heather and Myron and Charles. Of course Mary don't go to school yet, but she'll be starting next year."

So, there I was, face to face with the raw material of my trade. The boys were smaller duplicates of their father, manure-stained moccasins, patched overalls, ragged homemade haircuts, and all. Of the girls I remember only skinny legs, much-darned brown stockings, faded cotton dresses, long stringy hair, and pinched white faces. In those hungry years, even farm children were undernourished.

Somewhere along the line I had formed a mental picture of my first public appearance as a pedagogue. Children and adults alike, I supposed, would be awed and deferential. I would be suave and rather jolly. There would be laughter and warmth.

It wasn't like that at all. Mrs. McDougall and the children just stood and stared at me with a mixture of resentment and hostility. I was a nuisance to one and all. To the children, because it meant beginning school again. To the elders, because they had to do something about me and, as a stranger, I accentuated their wretched condition. I smiled weakly and made an attempt at small talk, but their inscrutable stares got to me, and I gave up.

Then Mrs. McDougall took a coal-oil lamp from the table and led the way to a back bedroom with wooden walls and a slanted ceiling. There was a wash-stand and an iron bed covered with a thick feather tick. I learned later that the bed normally held two of the McDougall children who for this night were sleeping with the two others crosswise on a bed. I put my coat on the bed, rinsed my hands and returned to the kitchen, carrying the lamp with me.

Supper of roast pork, potatoes, turnips, and preserved Saskatoon berries was eaten in silence. Afterwards there was nothing to do. The light was too poor for reading, and besides there wasn't a book or magazine to be seen. Nor was there any radio. So we went to bed.

Before going, McDougall nodded to me and stepped out the back door. I followed him, not knowing what he wanted. But I soon found out. As the two of us stood and aimed our streams into the snow on opposite sides of the path, I looked up where the stars shone like lamps and the northern lights slithered about in the sky.

The prairie sky has been described with fine terms like "majestic," "inspiring," and "awesome." To me it just looked big and unfriendly. I picked out the Big Dipper and the North Star, not realizing that before I was through with this place I would be using them as my only guides across snow-covered fields, and that when they weren't visible I would be hopelessly lost.

McDougall grunted something. We shook, buttoned, and went in.

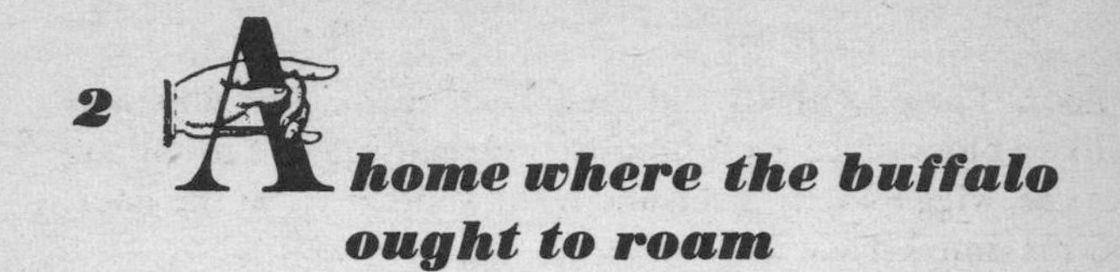

2 A home where the buffalo ought to roam

I didn't sleep well that first night in Willowgreen School District. The McDougall house was small and cold. There was no insulation in walls or ceiling and the house was heated, as were many prairie homes, by the kitchen range and a round ornate heater in the living room. Neither was kept burning all night. It just wasn't practical. McDougall had no coal to burn, and he couldn't be expected to stay up all night to shove wood into a stove.

Besides, who needs a fire at night? McDougall and his wife could certainly keep each other warm. The children slept together in their long, fleece-lined underwear and cuddled spoon style, generating enough heat for them. No provision was made for a visiting schoolteacher. Why should there be? He was something foreign in the body of this culture.

When I awoke in the morning it was pitch dark. I heard somebody in the kitchen clanging stove lids. Then I heard the kitchen door open and the sound of stamping feet. I knew it must be time to get up.

I slid my feet out from under the covers and onto the

floor. Then I quickly slid them back again. The floor was like a block of ice. By fishing around on the floor I found my socks, wiggled into them, and made another try at the floor. This time I made it.

I found my pants, got a match from a pocket, and lit the coal-oil lamp. In the pale yellow light I could see frost clinging to the inside of the wall. Hurriedly I scrambled into my underwear and pants and picked up the big white pitcher to pour out some water. None came. A quarter of an inch of ice covered the surface. It was the first, but not the last, wash and shave I ever had in ice water.

And now I became acutely aware of the most practical, universal, and insistent of all problems. I opened the door on the front of the wash-stand. It was empty. I got down on my knees and looked under the bed. Nothing there.

I sat on the bed and shivered. Where was it? I knew the house had no plumbing, but surely there was some sort of inside convenience. I could hear children's voices in the kitchen, and to march past them on such an obvious mission seemed a most unteacherish thing to do. Besides, I didn't know where to go when I got outside. I scraped the frost off a small patch of window pane and peered out. In the pre-dawn dusk I dimly made out a little cluster of out-buildings, half buried in the snow. One of them had a slanted roof. Maybe that was it.

The situation had deteriorated, as they say, to the point where something drastic had to be done. I pulled on my shirt, sweater, and boots and tiptoed over to the door. Gently I turned the knob and eased it open.

My timing couldn't have been worse. At that very moment McDougall came past the door, braces pulled over grey underwear top. "Oh, you're awake then," he grunted. "Come on. Breakfast is just about ready." I was trapped.

The four young McDougalls were already in their places against the wall. Feeling I should do something friendly, I smiled broadly and said something asinine like, "Well, well, how is everybody this morning?" They neither smiled nor nodded nor spoke. Just stared.

Since I couldn't outstare them, I looked at my plate and breathed a silent prayer for strength. Mrs. McDougall came into the room then carrying an immense white platter covered three deep with greasy fried eggs and salt pork. A plate of thick toast made from crumbly, homemade bread was already on the table. There was no butter.

Mrs. McDougall handed me the plate of eggs and I gingerly manoeuvred one of them onto my plate and passed the platter to McDougall. He grunted, tipped the platter over his plate, and slid off half a dozen eggs together with a pile of the pork. The children did the same when their turn came, filled their glasses with milk, and began to eat.

My appetite was poor. I shoved the egg around in the grease with my fork and took a few tentative nibbles at it. The coffee and milk I left strictly alone.

As McDougall shovelled the food into his mouth and washed it down with coffee, he seemed to be preoccupied. "Don't know where you're going to live," he finally mumbled, wiping the grease from his lips with the back of his hand.

This stunned me. I hadn't even thought of it, considering that, since they had brought me here, they would see to it that there was a home for me. "Where does the teacher usually board?" I asked.

"Smithwick's," McDougall grumbled. "Used to, before the trouble."

The kids began to giggle, and McDougall glared at them; they stopped.

"There's a teacherage in the basement of the school," Mrs. McDougall hurriedly explained.

"Fixed it up for Sado and that wife of his," McDougall grunted in disgust.

Again the kids giggled. Again he silenced them with a look.

It was like a game of missing words or missing sentences. You fill them in. Obviously there had been some trouble at Smithwick's, and there was something odd about Sado's wife, too. But I had troubles of my own.

"The teacherage is really quite nice," Mrs. McDougall went on. "There's a table and a cupboard and a range heater in one room and a nice big bed in the other."

I didn't know what a teacherage was, but I was getting the idea that I would be expected to live alone there and do my own cooking. Even that seemed insignificant to what I was enduring.

Then I had an inspiration. The kind of desperate inspiration a man about to be executed might get. "The teacherage sounds nice," I gasped, putting down my fork. "Could we go and see it now?"

"Now?" McDougall raised his eyebrows. "I thought we'd better talk about your money first."

"No, no. Never mind the money. Let's go and see that teacherage!"

McDougall stared at me for a minute in disbelief, then pushed back his chair and heaved himself to his feet. "All right, come on," he said. "I'll hitch the team."

While he was hitching the team, I'd reconnoitre the outdoors for the "thing". Quickly I got into my hat and coat and rubbers and followed him out the back door. The snow on either side of the path was a yellow-stained skating rink where Mrs. McDougall had been throwing the slops for the past three months. I hurried along towards the barn and spotted my little square house with the slanting roof. There was no path, and so I floundered through the snow and pulled the door open, frantically kicking away the snow to do so. Finally the door came open, and I saw inside. A drift two feet high lay on top of the seat.

By now my situation was critical. I turned and dashed through the snow to the barn door. This would have to do.

As I entered the barn I heard a voice, a small feminine voice. Mary McDougall had followed me. "Do you want to see our colt?" she asked. "We had two, but the other one died. Dad said it was just as well because there wasn't enough feed anyway."

Blast the kid! Why did she have to become communicative at this particular moment? I went and looked at the colt. And, by the time I'd seen it and the calf and the baby pigs, the team was hitched, and McDougall was waiting for me.

There was absolutely nothing in what we'd learned at Normal School to cover this most vital of all problems.

We drove along the winding trail away from McDougall's house. The sun was shining in a blue sky. A flock of tiny snowbirds flew past, looking like an undulating wave; they landed on a nearby fence and went to work on the seeds of the brown Russian thistle stalks piled against it. In the distance I could see the square schoolhouse sitting up on a cement foundation in the middle of a school yard that was in the middle of nothing. There wasn't another building or even a tree in sight in any direction.

McDougall stopped the team, produced a key, and let us in. "This is the main room here," he explained, opening another door, but I wasn't with him. I'd spied the cellar steps and taken them two at a time.

At the bottom there was an indoor chemical toilet. My agony was past.

The school was typical of many that had been built in the post-war, pre-depression years when the price of wheat had been good. It was about twenty-five feet square with windows all along one side. Except for a small cloak room and closet at the entrance, it was all classroom. A blackboard, made of wall board covered with shiny black paint that was chipped off in places, extended across the front and part way down the side. In the right front corner stood an ancient organ, brown walnut with its top scarred round the edges by hundreds of butts of roll-your-own cigarettes left there during dances by organists, fiddlers, and dancers.

A tattered map of the world, its oceans frilled with bright pictures of candy bars, products of the company who supplied it free, was on the side wall beside the blackboard. Above the blackboard at the front a two-foot-long Union Jack was held in place by thumb tacks. On the back wall was a picture of King George V. Below it was a hole in the plaster where it had been hit by a flying book or body. In front of the hole was a large glass water cooler, fitted on a stand so as to make a drinking fountain. I didn't know it then, but this thing was to haunt my dreams.

The seats and desks arranged in six rows were of the kind that can be adjusted up and down, forward, back, and slantwise, but, no matter how you adjust them, never fit the sitter. They could also be moved, either by the occupant kiddie-car style, or over to the side wall when the room became a dance hall or political auditorium. As desks they were of doubtful value, but as noise-makers they were without rivals. The large drawer underneath each seat, for instance, always stuck, so that it could be opened only with a mighty heave. Then it came all the way out with a thump and a clatter that could wreck the strongest nerves.

At the front of the rows of desks, dead centre, was the teacher's desk with a small shiny hand bell on top of it.

McDougall waddled over and tapped the bell with a chubby finger. Then he pulled open the flat top drawer where I could see the brown cover of a register book. He fished around with his hand and finally located a piece of belting about two feet long and three inches wide. "Strap," he grunted. "Better get used to using this, because there's some pretty big kids in Grade Ten."

I stood behind the desk, looked down at the empty ones

in front of me and the gaping hole in the plaster, and for the first time felt absolutely alone, helpless, and scared. I'd taken the bleak station, the long, frost-bitten ride, and McDougall's cold house, and even the strain on my bladder with a certain aplomb. But the sight of this bare, untidy, desolate room where I would spend most of my waking hours was almost too much.

McDougall hunched his ragged mackinaw around his shoulders, muttered something about nothing being colder than an empty building, and led the way through the door at the back of the room and down the basement steps. They were steep and narrow with a right-angled turn half way down. "Watch your head," he warned, ducking his own to miss the floor joist as he went past.

I'll never forget that basement. In retrospect it has become the Black Hole of Calcutta, the Moose River Mine, and a bottomless pit, all rolled into one. I think it was the darkness of it. The school had no electricity, of course, and I rarely took a lamp into this room which was dominated by a huge galvanized-iron coal furnace with an enormous hot air pipe going out the top and an enormous cold air pipe coming in the bottom. The chemical toilets, one for the boys and one for the girls, were under the stairs (those indoor toilets made up for a lot), and the coal bin was at the other side.

This was half the basement. The other half was partitioned off to make the teacherage McDougall had mentioned earlier. It consisted of two rooms, each twelve and a half feet long and about eight feet wide, and each with a tiny basement window near the ceiling. The living room had a table, a kitchen chair, and a heater-range, which was a Quebec heater with a kitchen-range-type top and an oven on the side. A coal-oil lamp with a dirty chimney sat on the table, its long grey wick curling down into the oil in the glass bowl like a grey tapeworm. The other room had a bed of sorts, without head or foot, and a wash-stand with a blue and white porcelain basin with a crack running across its bottom and up each side, and an immense water pitcher of the same design with its handle broken off, sitting in the centre of it. There was no other furniture.

McDougall stood in the middle of the room, hands in mackinaw pockets, shoulders hunched. "Well?" he asked.

"Is there a boarding place?" I asked. "Besides Smithwick's, I mean?"

"Well, not exactly. Nobody else wants to take the teacher full time, but some has agreed to take you month about."

"How would I get to school?"

"Walk. Or ride with the kids, if there is any."

"Why can't I stay at one place instead of moving around?"

"Well . . ." he looked around for a place to spit, found none, opened the door and splattered tobacco juice out on the floor of the basement proper. "It's a question of taxes. Work 'em off that way."

"I don't quite understand."

"They's not enough cash money around now to buy a gopher trap. But the work of the municipality's still got to be done . . . roads graded . . . weeds cut . . . coal hauled to the school here . . . miserable jobs like that. Everybody does some. Get a tax credit for it."

"I see." Then I grinned as though we shared a secret joke. "And boarding the teacher is one of the miserable jobs."

He didn't grin. "Some folks might call it that."

I gulped and sat on the one chair. "Perhaps we'd better discuss salary after all."

He heaved his big rump onto the corner of the table. "Can't pay much, and that's a fact. I hear they's getting teachers – experienced ones, too – in the other districts for four and five hundred. One south of the river got a teacher for three. You ain't got no experience, I understand."

"No. Except, of course, practice teaching at Normal."

"Yeah. Well . . . in a sense you're sort of learning on the job, as they say. We'll provide you with a place to live, grub to eat, and a little cash money besides. It's a hell of a sight more'n a lot of farmers with thirty years' experience are getting right now."

"If I decide to stay here, how can I buy food?" I asked.

"People in the district will bring it. We got plenty eggs. We can send them over with the kids. Haven't any extra milk though, so somebody else will have to provide that. Maybe MacLean. He had a cow freshen last month. We'll see you don't starve."

I was thinking of my thin overcoat and riding to school every morning in a cutter or even walking. Besides, with the pride of youth, I was thinking of my limited wardrobe and my inability to buy more. Living alone here, I wouldn't need to disclose the state of my underwear or to buy the new suit I'd planned with my first pay cheque.

"I guess I'll stay here then," I mumbled.

McDougall turned and started out the door. "I'll let the others know," he said. "The women'll come over on Saturday and clean up the place and bring stuff."

I followed him up the steep wooden steps from the basement and out the door into the clear bright sunlight. While he untied the team from the gate post, I looked around. Not a house or a tree visible in any direction. Just the rolling prairie land covered with snow, broken here and there by a barbed-wire fence clogged with Russian thistle.

A lead weight settled in the middle of my stomach. This desolate, wind-swept barrens was to be my home. Here I would learn what isolation means and what it can do to the soul.

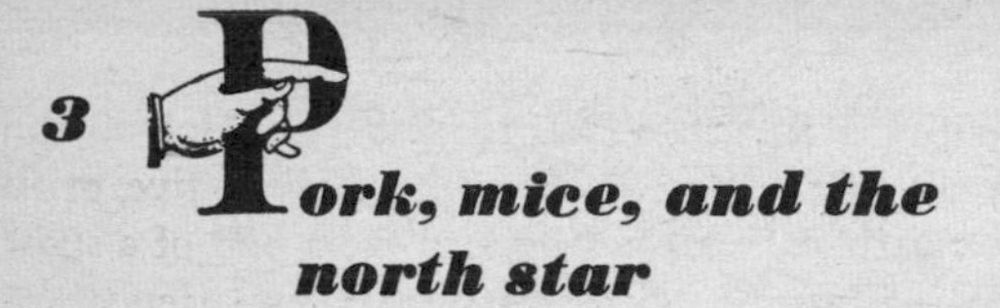

3 Pork, mice, and the north star

It's frightening how much we take for granted. All my life I had been used to having plenty of people around (when you're one of a family of eight you're rarely alone, waking or sleeping), somebody to keep house for me, water in taps, light in bulbs, and well-marked streets. Now, finding myself with none of these things I was pretty helpless. Without companionship I was hit by a deadening lethargy; without a housekeeper my living conditions degenerated into chaos; and without well-lighted streets to guide me I almost ended my teaching career before I began it.

When I arrived at the school the next morning (on foot; McDougall had done his duty by driving me once and wasn't about to do more), I found my main room filled with women and food. The women were of varying builds from short and scrawny to big and buxom, and all wore that haggard look of women who have worked too hard and too steadily. The food covered my table and most of the floor.

In the middle of the table were two round, knobby-sided, brown-topped loaves of home-made bread, a dish of pale yellow butter, a carton of eggs, a slab of home-cured bacon, a quart sealer half full of milk, a paper bag of sugar, a box of salt, and a can of pepper. On the floor, a sack of potatoes, a wooden box of withered carrots, some scurfy turnips, and – the pièce de résistance – a gunny sack containing two bushels of ground wheat.

This wheat was the real thing, nothing added, nothing taken away. All the bran, shorts, wheat germ, flour was there. Little Mrs. Field who had brought it explained shyly that it was good for making porridge. "You cook it for an hour or so in a double boiler," she said in an English accent that sounded strangely out of place amid the Western drawls. "You'll find it will stick to your ribs." She was absolutely right. It stuck to the ribs, the pan, the spoons, the stove lids. Like cement it stuck. And I ate it every morning while I was there.

But the hunk of food that dominated the entire collection was a quarter of pork. Mrs. Montgomery, who was large and dark-haired and wore moccasins and a faded blue sweater pulled over an enormous bosom, explained that her husband had lately killed a pig, and this was my share. I stared at it in awe. It was about three feet long, tapering from a cloven hoof at one end to a pail-sized slab of raw, red, quivering muscle at the other. I half expected it to jump off the chair on which it was crouching and run out the door.

"What do you do with it?" I asked helplessly.

"Cook it of course. And eat it."

"Cook it? But how?"

She realized then that she was talking to a city boy who knew about meat only what he saw in brown paper wrappings. No farm boy would have asked such a crazy question.

"I'll cut off a ham," she said, taking a huge butcher's knife and cutting into the meat about eight inches back from the big end. Then she sawed through the thigh bone and finished slicing. The result was a roast of pork that must have weighed twelve pounds. "Roast this in your oven," Mrs.

Montgomery instructed, "and you can eat it hot and then cold."

"What about the rest of the . . . the . . . thing?" I asked.

"Well, you could put it outside and freeze it. Then store it in the barn. Hang it up, of course, so that a coyote or weasel can't get at it..." I looked so helpless that she changed her mind. "No, I'd better take it home and can it for you."

"Can it?"

"In sealers. With the fat. It keeps very well that way." One of the other women had lighted a fire in the heater-range and the cold clammy feel was beginning to leave the room. Then they swept the floors and scrubbed them, washed off my shelves and covered them with fresh sheets of the *Western Producer*, put clean sheets on my bed, pointed out the cream can of water that Leonard Stevenson had brought and the slop pail under the table, and left.

I was alone, completely and utterly alone. The only sound down there was the low murmur of the fire and the creaking of the boards as the frost left them. From upstairs I could hear the rhythmical ticking of the big old wall clock echoing in the empty schoolroom. A heavy, unaccountable pain settled in my mid-section.

Following Mrs. Montgomery's instructions, I shoved the mammoth chunk of pork into the oven and opened the draughts. This was a mistake. The purpose of a Quebec heater-range is to produce heat while baking, and a good one can heat a five-room house. In my cramped quarters the result was devastating. Soon the temperature rose to over a hundred degrees Fahrenheit and opening the little windows did no good. I had to get out.

When I came back two hours later, after wandering about the room upstairs and looking out the windows at nothing, my kitchen was filled with the succulent smell of roast pork. My appetite came on with a rush and I prepared my first meal – and, I guess, my best – in Willowgreen

School. I peeled and washed enough potatoes for a family of ten, fixed carrots to match, boiled them up, sliced half a dozen pieces of the fresh bread, cut off a half-inch thick slab of the white steaming pork, and sat down.

Then my appetite deserted me. Never before in my life had I come to a meal completely alone. Always there were at least half a dozen others to argue with, laugh with and compete with for the biggest piece of pie. And now, having been alone for only half a day, I was reduced to a feckless blob of self-pitying apathy. I sat staring at my food for a few minutes, nibbled a bite or two, and left it there. Of all the horrors of living alone, eating alone is the worst.

I took the coal-oil lamp whose chimney had been left sparkling by the ladies but which was now showing signs of soot, and wandered up the stairs into the schoolroom. The black windows gave back my dim, sad reflection. Shading the lamp with my hand and pressing my nose against the glass I peered out, but there wasn't a light of any kind in sight. Then I set the lamp on a desk and went out into the cold night, walked a short distance from the school and looked in all directions. Still not a light to be seen. Far off a lonely coyote lifted his grizzled muzzle to the sky and howled mournfully.

With an ache in my mid-section that I still get when the family is out of sight for more than an hour, I went back into the school and downstairs to my rooms. I nibbled a little more of the cold meal and left it. There was no point in unpacking my trunk. The shirts and underwear and one sweater and extra pair of pants I owned would be just as happy there as hanging on nails stuck in the beaverboard wall. I didn't own a suit of clothes.

There was nothing to do. Not a magazine to read, not even a weekly newspaper. Anything as ostentatious as a radio was out of the question. There was no aerial on the schoolhouse and besides, radios then needed a complicated set of "A" and "B" batteries that required regular charging. I had brought a fair number of books, but after reading for a while by the pale yellow flickering flame of the coal-oil lamp, I gave that up.

So, I did what the farmers did in winter, went to bed early. And then the little rooms that had been so silent gradually filled with tiny noises. A spoon rattled on the table. I went tense. Could the place be haunted by the ghosts of schoolmarms who had perished here of loneliness? The sound of scampering feet across the floor and a small panting near my head. And then the tell-tale squeak. The place was galloping with mice.

I got up and lit my lamp. Yep, there was the unmistakable evidence of my little visitors on the plate of food left on the table. Couldn't have that. I scraped the food into the slop pail and then rummaged in the table drawer for a mouse trap. I baited it with a piece of bread and set it on the ledge of my open window above the bed. Then I lay down.

Again the little noises in the dark, a loud snap, a short scuffle and something landed with a soft thud on my chest. A slight squirming and then all was still. I got up again, lit the lamp and inspected my prey. It was a deermouse, which must be the commonest mammal in North America, tiny and buff coloured with white belly and feet. His soft ears were very large and his black eyes bulged from their sockets, forced out by the stiff wire of the trap which had caught him across the forehead. His long whiskers quivered.

For a little moment I sat there on the edge of my bed stroking the soft fur of his back. Why had I killed him, a member of the only species of living creatures that wanted to share my home? I got up, walked across the room and plopped him into my slop pail. And I trapped no more mice. They made their nests in my other pair of shoes, drowned in half-empty milk sealers, nibbled vegetables, punctuated the top of my table with their leavings. But they kept me company, and so far as I was concerned they could stay.

The next morning, Sunday, I was up early. After porridge and eggs I took a deep breath and went up into the classroom. I sat down at the walnut teacher's desk, spread my hands out on its top, and felt like a man with a job. I inspected the register, placed the wastepaper basket where it should be, got out the chalk, tested the blackboard, and brought the tattered, musty-smelling readers and arithmetic books from the cupboard ready for use. Then I tried to study my Normal School notes, but it was no good. For the rest of the morning I made a pretense of working, then fixed a cold pork sandwich for lunch. I knew I couldn't stay in that place another second. I had to get out.

So, I did what I would be forced to do time and time and time again that winter – went visiting, unannounced and uninvited. McDougall had told me that Lyle English lived about a mile southeast of the school. As he was chairman of the school board I reasoned that I should pay him an official visit anyway. So, I walked across the hard-packed drifts of the school yard which took me over the top of the fence and climbed a slight knoll, from the top of which I could see for miles. There, across a stubble field and another that was in summer fallow, were the buildings of Lyle English's farm. White, L-shaped house with small garage beside it, red, big-roofed barn with two conical oat-sheaf stacks beside it, low machinery shed, tiny smokehouse, outdoor privy, and that was it. Not a single tree in sight.

About half way between the school and the farm stood a last year's straw stack with the bottom eaten away, so that it looked like a huge, white-capped mushroom. And huddling close to its hollow base were half a dozen long-haired work horses which had been turned out to forage for the winter. It was the only way they could be fed during their long period of inactivity, and the method also acted as a sort of natural control. The strong, healthy horses survived; the old, weak ones died and their carcasses were eaten by coyotes. It saved a lot of trouble.

I walked across the fields, into the yard and over a drift as high as the privy. There were no slop water stains around that back door. As I approached the door my natural shyness descended upon me and I lost my nerve. I'm all right at meeting new people when there are introductions, but introducing myself is worse than running into a burning barn. I hesitated and half turned to go back. Then I heard a sound I couldn't resist. A radio. I knocked on the door.

Mrs. English was tall and thin and neatly dressed. She had reddish hair done up in a bun and a sharp, reddish face. Behind her I caught a glimpse of a neat, tidy kitchen.

"You're the new teacher," she said matter of factly and without a smile. Then, before I could answer she went on. "Well, come in." Turned and lifted her voice. "Lyle, it's the teacher."

Lyle English came into the kitchen then. He, too, was lean, about forty years of age, and he was dressed in a pair of clean overalls. He held out his right hand and I saw that the second finger had been taken off at the middle knuckle. I've met a surprising number of farmers with one or more fingers missing, a natural consequence of all the plumbing, carpentry, blacksmithing, tinsmithing, and mechanical work they do.

"Hello, Teacher," he said and then stood and looked at me awkwardly. It's a wretched thing, but men who are warm and friendly and outgoing with other people become reserved and awkward when faced with a teacher or a preacher. I guess it's because they've all had teachers at one time or another and the image of an authoritative, forbidding person remains. Lyle English was the kind of man I would have liked to have had for a close friend, but I could see at a glance that it would never happen.

I followed him across the varnished linoleum, through

the dining room, and into the cozy living room. There was wallpaper and curtains, and a flowered rug on the floor. On the windowsill geraniums were in bloom. A huge pot-bellied stove standing on a metal mat in the centre of the floor was polished and gleaming. But best of all, on a high table against the wall sat a long, many-knobbed radio, and in a semi-circle in front of it, three easy chairs. Lyle English motioned towards one of them and I sank into it with a deep sigh of gratitude. This was the first really comfortable resting place my backside had found since I left home.

My host leaned forward, twisted a knob and the music stopped. "Did McDougall talk salary to you?" he asked.

"He mentioned four hundred and fifty dollars for the year, but that seems . . ."

"It's the best we can do." His face was hard. "Times have been bloody awful bad around here for four years now. Price of wheat's a disgrace. And cattle. God! I shipped ten steers to Winnipeg last fall and you know what I got for them? A bill. Yessir, by God, they didn't even bring enough to pay the freight."

I squirmed uneasily and tried my best not to feel responsible for this disgusting state of affairs.

"Of course," he went on, "you'll get the use of the teacherage as well. Let's see . . ." He took a stubby pencil from the bib pocket of his overalls and began to write. "Figuring that the year is ten months, that figures to $45.00 a month. But then we'll have to take off for the food folks are providing. That will figure at twenty-five a month. So . . . you'll have another twenty a month coming. Right?"

I nodded. It wasn't much, but then I had no place to spend it. In two months I could at least get a suit of clothes.

But that hope was short lived. "We can't give you any cash," Lyle English muttered. "We just haven't got any. You'll have to take a promissory note, and I'm damned if I know when we'll be able to make it good."

He reached up onto the table for a can of fine cut to-bacco, blew a paper loose from the small book of them, and proceeded to roll himself a cigarette. Then he shoved the can towards me, and I did the same. Each of us was thinking his own thoughts.

Mine were bitter. Forty-five dollars a month for taking full charge of and responsibility for a school full of pupils. Hired men were being paid more, and their board thrown in with it. But good hired men weren't as plentiful as teachers. English knew, and I knew, that if I turned down the job he could have another teacher out here in two days.

He tucked loose tobacco into his cigarette, twisted the end, and looked at me. "Well?"

Well, indeed. What could I do? I didn't have a dime in my pants to buy a train ride back to Saskatoon. And there was nothing there but a city full of unemployed and a house full of bickering. But inside me an anger smouldered like coals smouldering in a furnace, never bursting into flame, but never dying out either.

Lyle English extracted a bullet-shaped lighter from his pocket, removed the top and rubbed the wheel with his thumb, producing a flame about three inches high. Twisting his head sideways, he held the flame to his cigarette and sighed in a deep draught of smoke. And when he spoke there was anger in his voice. A deep quiet anger at whatever had brought him to this. For he was a proud man, proud and hard working.

"McDougall has the contract," he said. "You can sign it when you get the chance."

Then he got up and twisted the knob of the radio. A female with a deep voice was singing that just around the corner there was a rainbow in the sky. Lyle English snorted and twisted the dial again. From Denver a commentator stated in clipped tones that "when Roosevelt takes office in

March, it seems likely that we can look for far-reaching changes."

I noted then something I was to note many times during subsequent uninvited visits to the English home. When he touched his radio knobs, Lyle English did so with something akin to reverence. And well he might. The radio was his concert hall, sports arena, public forum, newspaper. It was more. It was his contact with the world of sport which he loved above all else. Sitting beside that long walnut box, he could be thousands of miles away. In Yankee Stadium watching a World Series game, at Madison Square Gardens marvelling at the artistry of Barney Ross, at Churchill Downs cheering Top Flight in the Derby.

Lyle English knew more baseball than many sports writers I've met since. Although he'd never been in a major-league park, he could quote the World Series batting averages of every player in the American or National league, past and present. He yarned about Pepper Martin and Connie Mack as though he had ridden the buses and trains with them for years. Discussing baseball he became a new man. The lines of fatigue, worry, and frustration left his face. Even his voice changed. He chuckled and smiled and rubbed his hands together and lived. The overworked phrase, "magic of radio", had real meaning on the prairies in the thirties. It was the beginning of the end of the soul-killing isolation.

While we listened to the radio Mrs. English prepared dinner. I was very much aware of the clatter in the kitchen and her footsteps in the dining room as she set the table. No one had said anything about me staying for a meal, and I had an uneasy feeling that if I got up to leave they would let me go. But I couldn't do it. Couldn't find the strength to leave that comfortable chair and the sound of the radio. So I just stayed where I was. And, when Mrs. English finally announced that dinner was ready, I got up and walked to the table like any member of the family. The two English children, Betty aged thirteen and Carl, fifteen, appeared from somewhere and were introduced to "the teacher". We all sat down to a delicious meal of roast pork.

After dinner it was the same thing. While coal burned in the large heater, throwing a flickering glow through the tiny mica squares of its door, we sat in a semi-circle and laughed at the jibes of Eddie Cantor and Rubinoff and his violin. Good entertainment can always take me completely out of myself and whatever condition I'm in, no matter how miserable it may be. But when it was over and the ten o'clock news had been read, it was time to face reality. And reality was two basement rooms, empty and forlorn except for mice, dirty dishes, and an enormous hunk of cold pork.

Lyle English went with me to the back door. It was a clear night, no wind, 25 below zero and a sky full of stars. The dim light from the lamp threw a feeble glow out over the snow, but beyond that it was black as the inside of a cave.

"Think you can find your way back all right?" Lyle English asked.

"Uh . . . I . . . yeah . . . sure."

He pointed skyward. "There's the Big Dipper, see. And there's the North Star. Just keep it off to the right at a forty-five degree angle. Go to the corner of the barn there, and through the gate. It's open. And remember, keep the North Star in the same place. You'll come to the school."

I thanked him for the directions and again for the supper. He grunted and shut the door.

Walking in the dark is a weird experience the first time you try it. All the little rises and hollows catch you off guard and you stumble a lot. I missed the opening between the stack and the barn and ran face first into the butt end of an oat sheaf. Away from the yard I tried to keep the North Star in its proper place as I groped my way across the summer-fallow field. Then a bad thought hit me. Suppose I missed the schoolhouse. What was a forty-five degree angle anyway? I didn't have a protractor in my pocket. A fraction of a degree off and I could go right past the schoolhouse. Besides, I wasn't too sure about the North Star. The Big Dipper I could see, and the two pointers. Diagrams I half remembered from my Trail Ranger manual showed these stars pointing to a big, bright star all alone in the sky. But this sky was cluttered with stars and none looked much brighter than the others. I picked out what seemed to be the brightest and plodded on.

It was very cold. My ears and cheeks were stinging and I had to keep taking off my mitts and rubbing them. Then my fingers would freeze. The cold seeped through my threadbare overcoat, and I could feel it all over my body.

There was nothing to do but keep on walking. So, I stumbled on, occasionally changing direction because of a hummock or knoll, and then trying to correct my course. Once I fell down. I had no idea of distance. Had I gone a quarter of a mile or half a mile? I began to panic. In just this simple stupid way, I realized, did people get lost and freeze to death. If I missed that schoolhouse, I might walk for hours without coming to another building. And I couldn't walk for hours.

Then, like a ship coming out of the fog, a huge figure loomed in front of me. I gasped in terror. A snort of alarm and the sound of galloping hooves. One of those damned horses. I stopped dead, panting and sweating in spite of the cold. Then, ahead and to the right, something somehow darker than the over-all darkness – a building-sized shape. Not the schoolhouse; the strawstack.

But it was on the wrong side of me. Desperately I tried to make a calculation, but my thinking was muddled by fright. For a silly moment I thought of curling up in the straw, but luckily I gave up that idea.

I walked on, the terror in me so great that I ignored the stars and went by instinct. The schoolhouse had to be out there somewhere in the dark. It had to be. But every knoll felt like every other one.

Ever since that night I've been convinced that there's a special guiding angel who, when the caprice is on him, steps down and takes the hands of fools. There is no other way to explain why, stumbling and bumbling my way over that frozen snow, I finished up with my belly against the corner post of the school yard.

A few moments later, sitting on the side of my bed and still shivering with cold and dread, I did some thinking. This was obviously no place for weaklings. Lyle English had let me out into the night without benefit of road or street lamp, not because he was careless of my safety, but because he just naturally figured any adult male could find his way home. Any child could have done as much. Or, for that matter, any dog or horse.

Tomorrow I would face the children.

4 First day

I awoke early that fateful Monday morning after sleeping badly and dreaming about children twice as big as I who wouldn't do a thing I said.

As soon as my feet hit the floor I knew the Quebec heater had gone out. I shuffled out into the basement proper and the furnace was out, too. I warmed myself up nicely splitting kindling and getting them going. That's one thing about the old style wood and coal burners. They may not throw much heat, but you surely do work up a sweat getting them started.

I went up the narrow stairs and looked out the window and immediately wished I hadn't. It was an extra miserable day, and in a country that specializes in miserable days, this is saying something. Dirty grey clouds hung low. A thirty-mile-an-hour northwest wind whipped snow around the corner of the school and through the crack in the window. The countryside lay bleak and cold with weed stems, out-buildings, and fences all leaning away from that persistent wind.

I stumbled back downstairs to put the porridge on and

discovered that both furnace and heater had gone out. I stood in the middle of the room and swore.

Nobody under the age of thirty-five can appreciate what the invention of the finger-tip control oil or gas burner has meant to people living on the North American plains. Beside this achievement, the invention of television or nylon stockings or even the atomic bomb are nothing. For there was no more diabolical, fiendish, cunning, dirty contraption than the coal-burning furnace. It was fickle as a woman, cantankerous as a mule, and very sensitive to heat and cold. Try to light a small fire on a moderately chilly day and immediately it caught and roared and glowed until you had to throw open all windows and doors. But let the temperature get down below minus ten and it sulked and sputtered and produced more smoke than a steam locomotive along with a BTU rating roughly equal to that of a candle.

Finally I got both the monsters going and put my porridge on to boil. But, since the wind was drawing ninety per cent of the heat up the chimney, it took time.

In my confusion, I'd forgotten to heat water and so I hurriedly shaved in cold. If I ever had the inclination and opportunity to avenge myself on an enemy who'd wronged me shamefully, I can think of no worse torture than forcing him to shave in cold water. To make matters worse, I sliced the top off a pimple on my chin and couldn't stop the bleeding.

I slicked my unruly hair back with vaseline hair tonic and dressed in my best clothes. That is, I put on the pair of freshly pressed trousers that I'd kept in the tray of my trunk for this great occasion, a faded blue shirt on which my mother had turned the collar, one of my older brother's discarded ties, and an almost-new blue cardigan sweater.

Then I went up the stairs.

The three McDougall children had already arrived and

were standing, still wearing their ragged coats and toques and clutching their lunch pails in mittened hands, on top of the square floor register. To be accurate, they didn't all have mitts. Little Heather, making her first appearance at school, had her hands covered with a much-darned pair of her Dad's woollen socks.

I smiled at them, held my hand over the register and felt a small breath of warm air coming up. They didn't smile back but stared at me morosely, showing me that I'd let them down by not having the place warm for them.

The sound of harness outside took me and the McDougalls to the window. The Stevenson children had arrived by team and sleigh with half a dozen others they picked up on the way. While Jake Stevenson drove the team to the barn and unhitched them, the rest came in and crowded around the register. Then Jake came in, lugging a five-gallon cream can. He set it on the floor, took the glass water cooler from its stand, turned it upside down and filled it, and set it back on the cooler.

Only then did he acknowledge my presence. "Pa says you can use the water that's left over for your cooking and that."

I started to thank him, but he'd already picked up his can and gone back out to the sleigh with it.

Gradually the others arrived and took up their places near the register. There was no talking, no laughter. Now and then they looked my way like prisoners sizing up a new guard.

At nine o'clock sharp I rang the bell. The children took off their outdoor clothes and sat down in the seats. And now they were in front of me, nineteen of them, ranging in ages from six to seventeen.

Seated in the row of small seats furthest from the window were four beginners, virgin soil in which I could sow seeds of wisdom. Not one of them could read a single word or count to ten. One could scarcely talk. In the next seat sat little Pearlie Sinclair, seven years old, but it was difficult to understand how any child could have got that dirty in seven years. She was skinny, wispy haired, rickety, and so terribly undernourished that it made one weep to look at her. Some days her lunch consisted of so little that I would bring food up from my own store to give to her.

In the next row was Myron McDougall, a chubby, freckle-faced kid who was to give me more trouble than all the others put together. Each year he'd been promoted into the next grade and he couldn't read a word. But he could recite, word for word, every story and poem in the first three readers. Take any word from those stories out of context and he couldn't read it. As I say, Myron presented a problem in pedagogy that would tax the science of an expert.

Sammy Sinclair had parked himself in the front seat of the Grade Five and Six row, but I soon moved him to the back seat. Like his little sister, he was dirty. And he had a skin ailment, common on the prairies then, called scabies or, more familiarly, "the seven years' itch". A great deal of nonsense has been said about teachers cleaning up their students. It would have been impossible with the Sinclairs. Nothing short of a bath at least once a week would do it, and I scarcely had enough water to give myself a bath once a week.

But I'll always remember Sammy Sinclair for what was certainly my most embarrassing moment in any school. As time went on, we organized a "School Civic League", which was described in the curriculum as an excellent means of teaching the principles of democracy through practice. All the officers were elected in the regular way and all business conducted strictly according to parliamentary procedure. One of the activities of the League was a school newspaper, written and edited by the students and read at the conclusion of each Friday afternoon's meeting. There were stories about school hockey games, fiction, poems and so on. And always a page of riddles for the little kids.

As I sat dozing in the back seat listening to this being read by the editor one Friday afternoon, I was suddenly brought to attention, too late, by this joke submitted by Sammy Sinclair and included in the paper by an older editor who certainly knew better:

TEACHER: *What is an island?*
PUPIL: A piece of land completely surrounded by water.
TEACHER: *What is a sea?*
PUPIL: A piece of water completely surrounded by land.
TEACHER: *What is a beach?*
PUPIL: A dog completely surrounded by other dogs.

My head came up with a start to find all the kids twisted around in their seats grinning and snickering at me. I did and said the only thing I could. Nothing.

Behind Sammy, later to be moved up to the front seat, was the sunniest little girl in the school. "Sunny" is the only word that adequately describes her. She was always clean and neat, her hair ribbon was always fresh and newly pressed, her stockings darned and her shoes polished. And she was nearly always smiling. Her parents, the Littlewoods, had named her Summer, and she truly brought a feeling of it into that bleak schoolhouse.

Behind her, Mary Field, the lone Grade Six student, was a silent, sombre child who rarely spoke and scarcely ever smiled.

In the next row were the Four Horsemen. Four boys in Grade Seven and Eight; all about the same size and the acknowledged leaders of the school. They set the mood. If you had them with you, you were all right; against you and the going could be rough indeed. I remember them as being all of a size and the same square build, with patched overalls, manure-spattered shoe packs, rough work shirts and tousled hair. Tough, cocky, brash, in the small community of Willowgreen School Jake Stevenson, Charlie McDougall, Bob Sanderson, and Bill Field constituted the nearest thing to a gang.

In the last row was my biggest class, Grade Nine. Five young people of serious mien and intent. The tone of this row was set by Betty and Carl English who sat in the first two seats. Betty was a year and a half younger than her brother, but he'd run into some bad health along the way and she'd caught up to him. Academically, they were about equal. Behind Carl was Paul Friesen, a Ukrainian boy, neat, precise, with a brilliant mind. Violet Sinclair and Jean Stevenson completed the grade.

At the back of this row, all by himself, sat the biggest boy in the room, Alan Littlewood. Like his little sister, he was usually smiling or asking a question in a slow, serious drawl. About an inch taller than I, he was long of limb and loose of joint. He was also one of the strongest boys I've ever known, and sometimes amused the younger children by galloping around the schoolyard with a couple of them clinging to his back.

There they sat, looking to me for wisdom, enlightenment, knowledge, growth. I don't know how other teachers feel when they look down at their first class, but I know how I felt – hopelessly inadequate and scared. Here I was, equipped with a senior matriculation and eight months in Normal School. And there they were, filled with God knows what mental quirks, neuroses, and attitudes bequeathed to them by parents, associates, and an incredibly harsh environment. I was their only hope; the influence of my stay there would remain with some of them a lifetime. I felt like a callow pup sent to do the job of a trained sheep-dog.

I jingled the little hand bell on my desk. "Class, stand!" I said in tones that I realized were an attempt at a distillation of the tones of all teachers I'd ever had. "We'll repeat the Lord's Prayer."

That first day was one of complete confusion, but somehow the clock got around from nine to three-thirty. Then the children scrambled into their outdoor clothes, grabbed their lunch pails and tore out the door like horses leaving a corral.

And when the door had banged behind the last of them and that sudden deadly silence settled on the room, loneliness cut into my vitals like a knife. I went to the window and watched them go, down the winding trail in the snow, out of sight. Then I heaved the heavy water cooler off its stand and, hugging it to my bosom, staggered down the steep steps with it to my dismal little grey home underground. Until the children came back the next morning, I realized I wouldn't see another living creature or hear a sound save the ticking of the big clock and the scurrying and squeaking of the mice.

But I had work to do. Somehow I had to figure out how to fit an average of eight subjects each for nine grades into a twenty-five hour week. Eight times nine are seventy-two, and twenty-five divided by seventy-two comes to less than twenty minutes per subject a week. And, considering that the beginners needed almost constant attention just to learn to read, the task became formidable.

5 The young idea

"To fit the individual to live and to function in the institutional life of his day."

This statement on the purpose of education kept bouncing about in my head. We'd had to memorize it at Normal School along with the bit about all learning being specific. But how, I wondered when I faced my first class, was I to achieve this in Willowgreen School?

In the first place these children could function pretty well already. From the smallest to the largest they could milk cows, feed them, clean out the barn, harness and drive horses, burn Russian thistle, plough, plant, and harvest. From their mothers the girls learned how to sew and bake and even how to deliver babies. The one bitter lesson they had to learn and I couldn't teach them was how to exist without funds in the harshest climate in the world.

But I realized that even in that small group there would be some who didn't want to be farmers. Who had a compulsion to get out of this mess into an environment where people lived like human beings. How about them?

For many years the old cry "Go West, young man" had

been completely reversed so that New York, Toronto, Boston, and other eastern cities were filled with young people from the West seeking careers in journalism, advertising, drama, broadcasting, and business. How could I help prepare them to fit into this world of culture, competition, and status seeking?

To complicate my problem the "modern trend" in education had finally seeped up to Saskatchewan so that the Department of Education had made extensive changes in its curriculum. The history courses, for instance, had been completely transformed to put more emphasis on living than on dying. Instead of nice, clean-cut facts about wars and generals and kings, such as I'd learned in public school, I was supposed to teach about such vague things as the development of towns, fairs, and guilds. And it wasn't to be called by the opprobrious name of History any more. Combined with Geography it had become Social Studies.

Similarly other subjects had been mutilated. Instead of notes to be dictated, copied, and memorized there was all this nonsense about projects and research. To further compound my confusion, no textbooks had yet been produced to cover the new approach. I had to get by with a tattered set of readers, some spellers, and the good old Elementary Arithmetic, parts I and II.

The library consisted of a book by James Oliver Curwood, a big tome called *Beautiful Joe's Paradise* and, of all things, a green-covered volume entitled *White Slavery – The Horrible Traffic in Young Women.* I removed it from the collection.

I solved the problem in the only practical way possible. After a couple of hours of futile fussing over a time-table that would include all the subjects for all the grades, I chucked the whole business and decided to teach reading, writing, and arithmetic. Naturally, the four beginners who couldn't read or write a word were my first, biggest, and most challenging task. What I did with them in Grade One would affect their whole school career. So I gave them about one-third of my teaching time.

And how do you teach a child to read? Of course, almost any non-teacher can tell you that teachers are doing it all wrong. People who scarcely know the meaning of the word propound the benefits of phonetics over the word recognition method. Actually both methods are used in conjunction with each other, but no matter how you do it, teaching a beginner to read is the toughest job a teacher can have.

I found it terribly hard. In the first place I had no equipment. Whereas today the specially trained primary teacher has a great variety of aids including any number of good books graded to the proper word level, I was stuck with a piece of chalk, a scarred blackboard, some scribblers, and one tattered primer for each child.

The trick was to keep them from memorizing the stories in the primer and simply rhyming them off. So, after I'd got them to recognize the simple words within their experience – "dog", "cat", "hen", "pig" and so on – I had to make up sentences involving different combinations of those words and print them on the blackboard. Every day, new stories. It was a long, tedious business. Then, from the words they learned to recognize the letters that made the sounds (phonetics) and they were on their way.

The old green primer that was universally used then has long since been replaced, but it contained the perfect story for teaching farm children to read. I don't know who wrote the classic, "The Little Red Hen", but it has everything. First, a cast of characters familiar to every farm child – the hen, the dog, the cat, the pig. Then, there is adventure – no less than the discovery of a treasure. Not gold or diamonds or pieces-of-eight (whatever they are), but a grain of wheat, the staff of life, the universally desired good.

Motivation? The story is loaded with it. The Little Red

Hen wants to grow the wheat. Nay, she must grow it, or starve. What better motivation than that? Now comes conflict and complication. This lone, intrepid hero calls on her friends for assistance in her noble venture. They turn her down cold. "Not I" said the dog, "Not I" said the cat, "Not I" said the pig. Then the Little Red Hen said, "Then I will plant the wheat myself." And she did. The clear, cold, logical beauty of it!

The same sad tale was repeated when she needed help to cut, thresh, and grind the wheat and then to make it into bread. But she didn't give up. Not this hen. She did it all herself. Then, when those plump, brown loaves were ready for eating (I can still see them), who was there with mouths wide open? You guessed it. The same cat, dog, and pig. But now it was Little Red's turn. She didn't give them a crumb. What a climax!

And what fine, rugged truths to be learned from this story. That you can't trust your friends for help in times of need. That they will try to con you out of your goods. That perseverance and hard work lead straight to success. That those who don't work don't deserve to eat. Truly a story with guts. Not at all like the modern pap about Dick and Jane and Baby Sally who live on such a nice street in such a nice suburb and get along so well with everybody.

All things considered, teaching those beginners to read gave me more downright satisfaction than anything else I've ever done. They couldn't read a word when I began with them, and when I finished each could stand up beside his seat and read words and sentences and stories. That's the kind of progress you can see.

But finding something for them to do while I was busy with the other grades presented a real problem. Thank Heaven for plasticine! Each child had a tattered match box full of it and a piece of oilcloth to roll it on. After each lesson out came the sticky green stuff and they proceeded to model the animals featured in the lesson. The first time this happened, I found little Sarah Friesen with a perfectly proportioned pig. So amazed was I that I almost asked her the silly question "Did you make this yourself?", until I realized that it would be equally amazing if her neighbour had done it for her. Her skill at drawing turned out to be equally startling. From what far-off ancestor had such a talent come?

And at the conclusion of each number-work lesson they took out their little post-shaped pegs, coloured green and red, and practised counting or whatever else took their fancy. Sometimes I'd glance over and see a tired head resting on a skinny arm and the weary, undernourished owner fast asleep. This was the best seat work of all.

Just moving across the room from grade to grade, reader to reader, took up the full morning. Most of the afternoon went in the same way with arithmetic. For reading and arithmetic are two subjects on which you can't skimp without bad trouble later.

What about the other subjects? Well, my stolen encyclopaedia took care of them. I'm not fool enough to divulge the name of this set of books (I don't want to get a bill at this late date) but I will say that they are the finest ever printed.

And right here I'd like to say a word for encyclopaedias in general and for the men who reap calumny for their efforts to sell them from door to door. The value of a good encyclopaedia to a family is second only to that of good parents. "Look it up," is the best counsel an inquisitive youngster can get from an oldster. Which is larger, New York or Tokyo? Look it up. What is a crustacean? Find out for yourself. Who was president following McKinley? It's in the book.

It is also a fact that few people go out and buy this handy home pedagogue of their own volition. Like insurance, books aren't bought; they are sold. And of all the hard things to sell in this world an encyclopaedia set is the hardest. A man who buys a new car every year, whose liquor bill runs into three figures, and who wouldn't be caught dead in a last year's suit, will kick a book salesman into the snow and be horribly indignant, because he may have been "taken" for a couple of hundred.

So, the encyclopaedia salesmen, or rather their mentors, must stoop to appealing to the customer's baser drives, his need for status ("We've selected a few prominent families to introduce this educational plan"), his greed ("We're giving it to you absolutely free"), his tendency to larceny ("In this way we get around the tax"), rather than telling him straight out that it's a good set of books and he should have it.

But to get back to my pilfered volumes. I still have them, and besides saving my life at Willowgreen School, they've been manhandled to tatters by my own five children. In the front fly-leaf is a statement to the effect that the purpose of the work is to inspire ambition, provide the inquiring mind with accurate information told in an interesting style, stimulate the imagination, and thus lead to broader fields of knowledge. Amen!

Besides all this, they are easy for any child of Grade Five or better to read and understand.

So, to fill the spaces between arithmetic, reading, spelling and grammar lessons, I assigned research from the encyclopaedia. The pupils looked up a subject, read what there was to read about it, and wrote a report. At first their efforts were pretty bad, but gradually they became surprisingly adept. Actually, each child spent about 80 per cent of his time working on his own. There's just a chance they gained in self-reliance more than they lost in lack of attention from me.

The encyclopaedia helped in another way. Spaced throughout the ten volumes were excellent nature stories for younger children. Often the senior students took a turn at reading these to the primary grades while I was busy elsewhere in the room.

As the great blob of confusion that characterized my first efforts gradually sorted out into some kind of order, I became acutely aware of Grades Nine and Ten. No new curriculum to worry about here. They were taking work that I'd taken myself only a few years previously and hadn't forgotten. Teaching them Math and French and History was easy and pleasant, but it was in Literature that I may have made that slight extra contribution for which a teacher is always striving.

A beginning teacher does what I suppose untrained beginners at any task must do: he tries to remember the best performer in the trade he's ever known and emulate his ways. So, my thoughts went back to an English teacher I'd had during my senior years in Saskatoon's Nutana Collegiate. He'd been a Rhodes scholar, was the author of several books, and loved literature so much that he'd spend part of his holidays memorizing Shakespeare.

His approach to a piece of prose or poetry was as a youth's approach to his first love – tender, reverent, filled with anticipation and excitement. He'd perch on one of the front desks and, his ruddy face beaming, begin in a fine deep voice to talk about the play, essay, or novel. Then he'd read some of the best parts to us, savouring them as a man savours good wine. And always he'd stop at the most tantalizing part so that we could scarcely wait to read the rest ourselves.

Thus, this fine teacher introduced me to Thomas Hardy, and before I was out of Grade Ten I'd read everything of his in the Saskatoon library, which was just about everything he'd written. Hardy's pessimism, preoccupation with the caprices of fate, and the suggested, rather than demonstrated, eroticism of many of his scenes were well suited to the mood of a poor boy confronted with the affluence of the twenties. Similarly he introduced me to Galsworthy, Wilde, Conrad, Lawrence, Wells, and Shaw.

Shamelessly I tried to copy the style and manner of this well-remembered teacher and do for these children what he had done for me. *As You Like It* was the play being studied in Grade Nine then and *Julius Caesar* was on the course for Grade Ten. So, I sauntered over to the outside row, parked my fanny on a rickety desk, gazed mournfully out over the frozen countryside, and, in a voice deep and dramatic, quoted:

"Blow, blow thou winter wind,

Thou art not so unkind

As man's ingratitude.

Thy tooth is not so keen

Because it is not seen,

Although thy breath be rude."

I paused and looked down at the class. Violet and Jean were staring at me with absolutely no expression. Paul looked startled and a little scared, as though he thought I might be violent. But in the faces of Betty and Carl English I detected the faintest spark of interest. And I felt the excitement a teacher feels once in a long time; the excitement at having lit a light that may grow into a prairie fire of interest, after which things will never be quite the same.

Encouraged, I launched into some more lines that I remembered and liked. This time I was more relaxed and so were the children. Then we talked about the old Globe Theatre and the excitement of the London playgoers who were lucky enough to be among the first to hear those lines.

And we speculated on that audience, out for nothing more than a good time, perhaps pleased with the wit of the play, perhaps disappointed because there wasn't enough bloodshed and raw sex. Then we began to read the play together. But soon I had to quit, because the eight other grades, although interested enough, weren't learning much. So back to Grade One I went, from the vicissitudes of Rosalind to those of the Little Red Hen.

That was the pattern of my teaching. From Grade One to Grade Ten and back again, by the shortest route. And in all their learning, scarcely a word about their own particular part of the world. "When I was down beside the sea, a wooden spade they gave to me . . ." But these children had never seen the sea, nor heard its roar. Poems and stories about babbling brooks, towering mountains, soaring larks, apples in orchards, the glory of the crimson maple leaf were lost to youngsters who had never seen these things. And not a word in all our reading about purple crocuses carpeting the prairie in spring, Hungarian partridges shooting out of the stubble like pellets from a gun, frozen sloughs covered with children on skates, wolf willow, gophers on the twine or the coyote's sad wail at night. Children living in a land without culture. Who never heard a symphony orchestra, saw a ballet or marvelled at an original painting. Whose idea of colour was the illustrations in Eaton's catalogue.

What did they get to make up for this lack? One thing. Toughness of mind and body. A boy who lives to maturity in that climate rarely feels cold anywhere else. He can take being wet and weary and frost-bitten. His lungs are strong, his muscles tough. And deep in his mind is the sure knowledge that to survive at all you've got to think faster and sharper and with more guile than the next fellow. He never has any doubt about life being a battle.

Are these lessons good? I don't know, but they are the ones they learn. Years later when the prairie schoolhouse was just a memory, while sitting in a bar in a large eastern city, I overheard a remark that gives an indication of what such experiences mean. At the table next to mine two advertising men were deriding a new colleague who was obviously overshadowing them. "Do you know what that s.o.b. did during the depression?" one asked the other in an outburst mixed with contempt and wonder. "He sold trees from farm to farm in Saskatchewan. Can you imagine it for chrissake!"

I couldn't help grinning to myself. Maybe there is some compensation in this crazy world after all.

6 The dance

Over the course of the years I've attended dances in posh wardrooms, army messes, and ballrooms twenty times as big as Willowgreen School. I've waltzed, rhumba'd and cha cha'd to small combos and big bands whose members are world-renowned musicians. But the dance that sticks in my mind for all time is the one in Willowgreen School when Orville Jackson played the fiddle and Grandma Wilson chorded on the organ.

I first got wind of it after school on Friday when, instead of slouching down the aisles making desultory passes at dust, Charlie McDougall and his band of helpers began by energetically pushing all the desks to the sides, back and front of the room.

"What's the idea?" I asked.

"Dance tonight."

"Here?"

"Yep."

"Who's coming?"

"Just about everybody in the district, I guess."

"Nobody said anything to me about it."

He merely shrugged at this and then, as an afterthought, "Oh yeah. Dad said to tell you they'll need your bed for the babies."

With that puzzling announcement he set to cleaning the floor as though he actually cared about getting the dust off it.

The bit about my bed bothered me to the extent that, after eating my supper of roast pork and bread, I got out the broom and swept my own rooms. Then I picked up the half dozen or so brown-stained cigarette butts from the edges of the table and shelves where they'd burned little black grooves. I even washed the dishes and the table top and put away the pork. Then I pulled the covers straight on my bed, hung my shirt on the back of the door and kicked dirty socks under the bed. The place looked almost tidy.

The Montgomerys were the first to arrive – and I had my first sight of Harris Montgomery who later was to become my mentor in socialism, adviser on morals, and instructor in the new economics. Seeing him then with the neat, if big, Mrs. Montgomery, I could hardly believe my eyes. He was the untidiest man I've ever seen, a sort of middle-aged beatnik. His eyes got me first, dark, wild and small beside the great bridge of his nose. Then the nose, sharp and hooked, extending down to his upper lip. His wrinkled face was lean, mouth slightly pointed, cheeks with shiny skin peeling from much exposure to wind.

He treated his wife always as a petty bourgeois and she treated him with that silent, tolerant contempt that wives have for husbands whom they've given up on.

When he saw me Harris Montgomery leaped forward, grabbed my hand, shoved his chapped face within six inches of mine, jabbed my chest with a nicotine-stained finger and demanded, "What do you think of Cole?"

"I don't know," I stammered. "I'm afraid I haven't met him yet."

"No, no, no, no! The Cole in England, I mean. The economist. G.D.H."

"Oh. That Cole?"

"Yes . . . yes. You've read him, haven't you?"

"Well . . . uh . . ."

"Great thinker. None of your mealy-mouthed bull manure about him. We'll have a talk about him. You live downstairs, don't you?"

"Well . . . yes."

"Good. We can go down there. Get away from all this damned falderal. I've been looking for somebody with some goddamned brains in his head to . . ."

But at this point Mrs. Montgomery captured him. "Hang up the Coleman," she commanded. "It's so puny dark in here, you can't see your hand before your face."

"Women!" Harris Montgomery muttered darkly. It was his most venomous expletive, and it summed up all the nonsense, muddled thinking and waste effort of the capitalist world.

But he'd lost this battle long ago. So he took a large gas lamp and hooked it on the end of a strong wire that extended down from the middle of the ceiling, and the whole room changed miraculously. I began to feel like a party.

"Now take these things downstairs." Mrs. Montgomery handed him a big wicker basket of provisions, and turned to her younger sister who came through the door carrying something bundled up in blankets. "You can put the baby downstairs on the teacher's bed. Is your fire going?"

"Uh . . . yes . . . yes, it is."

"Good. Harris, get that wash-boiler of water out of the sleigh and put it on the stove down there. And don't spill half of it on the way down the steps. Teacher, maybe you could help him."

With nothing more than my sweater on, I went out to the sleigh to help Harris with the water. As we did so another sleigh pulled by a team of ice-flecked Clydes came slanting dangerously over the drift at the gate.

"Wahooo!" A youth in a sheepskin mackinaw and no hat leaped out of the back of the sleigh, waving in his hand a mickey of gin. "It's a great night for the race!" he bellowed, crooking his arm over my shoulder and shoving the bottle at me. "Have a drink, pal."

Involuntarily I was reaching for the bottle when I heard Harris Montgomery's warning. "Cut it out, you damned fool Jake. That's the teacher!"

"Oh!" Jake, who was just about my age, sobered immediately. "Gawdamighty. I'm sorry, sir."

He shoved the bottle into his pocket, hurried off to unhitch the horses, and from the sleigh box came the sound of female giggles – young female giggles.

So, neatly and completely, I'd been categorized as "the teacher". Something from outer space, without feelings, Ichabod Crane. A nothing!

For a second I was swept by frustrated rage. Here was a party in my own place, and I couldn't even be part of it. Of course, if I'd had a jug of liquor hidden down in the furnace room or in the barn as the others did, I could have invited them for a drink. But I had neither the money nor the opportunity to get a jug, and even if I had, the news would have spread like a prairie fire that the new teacher at Willowgreen was a drinker. Not that he took a drink or was sociable or a good sport. Just a drinker, and who's going to send their kids to a school run by a drunkard, I'd like to know.

So they came, the old and the young, each with their bundles, many with babies. Some had come from as far as twelve miles, a three-hour journey over a winding snow trail. In the bottoms of their sleigh boxes they'd put stones, heated in the stove and wrapped in newspaper, for footwarmers. Some of the sleigh boxes were half filled with straw so that the children could snuggle down out of the wind like mice in a stack.

Why did they come? It was a break in the dreary drag of the winter months. They were sick to death of playing rummy and cribbage and of the sound of each other's voices. They'd had a bellyful of togetherness, babies, grandmothers, old-maid aunts, grown-up sons with no place to go, huddled in a few draughty rooms like foxes in a den, satiated with the sight and sound and smell of each other. This was their chance to break out for a few hours, see different faces, hear some gossip. Find out about that cow of Mark Brownlee's that was due to calf, the vicissitudes of fate, the shortage of feed, the uselessness of the Bennett nickel – a five-cent bonus on every bushel of wheat paid through the good offices of a prime minister who, like everyone else, was rendered confused and inept by the magnitude of the depression.

Soon the schoolhouse was full. My bed was covered with tiny bodies stacked across it like cordwood. Every so often a mother would come down the steps, listen at the closed door and, if she heard anything, tiptoe in and shove a soother into the mouth of the restless one. My kitchen-dining room was plugged with food, boilers for coffee, cups, plates and outdoor clothing. I had been dispossessed.

Upstairs were all the people in the district over the age of three. The very young squirmed on the laps of the very old. The little girls, with fresh hair ribbons and pressed print dresses, dashed about between their elders, chatted breathlessly, giggled, excited beyond comprehending by they knew not what. The little boys, on the other hand, hands shoved embarrassingly deep into knicker pockets, stood about not knowing quite what to do.

Almost to a man the male adults wore blue serge suits bought, heavens knows how many years before, through the Eaton's mail order catalogue. When the history of American costumes is finally written, the blue serge suit must surely have a special place as the worst fitting, the shiniest and most durable of all articles of clothing. Most of these were wedding suits and saw duty only at church, weddings, dances, Christmas concerts, and special political meetings. Some had been handed down from father to son to grandson.

The women, a half dozen of whom were in various stages of pregnancy, all had the same look of tired resignation. But, miraculously, as the evening progressed and the dancing became more animated, I was to notice this expression gradually change, the eyes regain a little of their sparkle, the cheeks a slight splash of colour and, from behind the tired, worried countenance, I got the occasional fleeting glimpse of what that face had been before the years – only a few, really – of drought and cold and worry and childbearing had cast them in the sad mould. The prairies are hard on women.

Of young girls there were only three. Two unbelievably homely and the other unbelievably beautiful. A dark-haired, round-cheeked, full-lipped, thick-bosomed girl whose shapely legs and thighs, which showed often as she was "swung out", made my mouth go dry and my loins ache just to see them.

It was a gay crowd, but I wasn't part of it. Mrs. Montgomery had made a few introductions, but they'd fallen flat. They mistook my natural shyness for a stand-offish attitude, and each attempt I made at light conversation came out all wrong. Finally I found myself standing around with my hands in my pockets, trying to keep out of people's way.

But I had my eye on the dark-haired beauty and I knew what I was going to do when the music started. I fancied myself pretty good at the flea hop, the foxtrot and the waltz, and could do a passable charleston. I'd show these damned yokels a thing or two. After all, I hadn't been nicknamed "twinkle toes" at Nutana Collegiate for nothing.

With a smattering of applause, the fiddler, Orville Jackson, took his place beside the organ in the corner. A short, bandy-legged man of about sixty-five, he wore a khaki peaked cap indoors and out. I soon discovered why. Most of his front teeth were gone and, in order to keep his pipe in his mouth while playing, he hung it from the peak of his cap by a thread. He cradled his fiddle in his left arm with the butt against his chest and began tuning it.

As he did so, Grandma Wilson, who must have weighed close to three hundred pounds, came forward and sank down on the organ stool, her ample bottom overlapping on all sides. She threw her beefy hands at the organ keys and came up with a wail like a sick cat. Orville tapped his right foot twice, waved his head gently back and forth so that the suspended pipe swung in time, and drew his bow across the fiddle.

Before I could even start towards the dark young lady, four young swains swooped down upon her and bore her off. Then I noticed that the music was almost completely unfamiliar and, instead of the dancers embracing each other and shuffling around the floor as I was accustomed to do, they arranged themselves in groups of eight, facing each other. A big florid man had taken his place beside the organ and bellowed, "Two more couples wanted"; then, when a grinning farmer and his six-year-old daughter had responded, "One more couple wanted."

Then I noticed a determined, red-faced matron approaching me and, before I could duck, she had me by the hand. "Come on, Teacher," she grinned. "Be my partner."

"Yeah, get in there and fight, Teach!" somebody shouted, and, as I looked around at their grinning faces, I knew that in some crazy way I was on trial. So I suffered myself to be led to the centre of the floor, which was by now so crowded that we could scarcely get through.

Then Grandma Wilson banged the organ, Orville Jackson sawed at his fiddle, the caller shouted in a great booming voice, "Places all!", and everybody began to move in different directions.

Now, it may seem strange, but although I was born and bred on the prairies, I had in my whole life not only never participated in a square dance, but I'd never even seen one done. As I recall it now, it was something like a football scrimmage and a basketball game combined. With women! As the music gained momentum and the caller bellowed louder and the stamping of feet became deafening, I became completely and hopelessly lost. I was shoved and pushed and chivvied about like a shopper at a bargain counter. Every so often one of the women would grab me and swing me around and then drop me. As I stomped aimlessly about I would regularly meet a six-footer in a red plaid shirt and face to match who'd take me by the shoulders with two immense hands and literally lift me into place, like a mother lifting a child. But I never stayed in place for long.

I remember once seeing an ancient book in which the evils of "round" dancing were deplored while "square" dancing was approved. This square dancing was not only indecent, it was downright perilous. Those muscular lads grabbed their partners by the nearest handle and swung them off their feet. Their dresses half the time flew up over their heads, and flying feet narrowly missed other people's jaws.

On and on, faster and faster went the dance until each couple had its turn doing whatever we were doing and then the music stopped. The panting, sweating participants sat down. My partner never even spoke to me, nor did any other member of the set. Whatever test I'd been put to, I had failed. Then the caller shouted his commands again and after a couple of "Two more couples wanted", the joint was jumping again. I can say this; that schoolhouse was mighty well built. Otherwise those dancers would have gone right through the floor and ended up in my quarters with their babies. As it was, the rhythm of the stomping feet shook the place till the desks rattled.

So it went on . . . and on . . . and on . . . square dance after square dance, with an occasional quadrille or schottische thrown in. Nobody invited me to dance again, and of course I didn't have the nerve to ask anybody. So I watched in a sort of terrified wonder as the others whirled and swung and pranced. Occasionally I caught a glimpse of my dark lady being pawed and patted and thrown about by rawboned hands, but I realized that there was nothing there for me.

When not dancing, the half-dozen young fellows stood in a group in the corner and told dirty stories. I knew a few that I thought they might not have heard, but when I wandered over to join them they stopped self-consciously and said nothing. I asked them if they'd heard the one about the camel who was raped by the monkey and they looked at each other in shocked amazement. When I told them how it had been accomplished, they didn't laugh but merely stared at the toes of their shoes ashamedly. What do you do when a joke falls flat on the floor like a piece of wet hay? I know what I did, I retreated awkwardly to a desk and perched on it. Shortly I was joined by a bewhiskered oldster who kept spitting tobacco juice on the floor behind the desks while he told me about his first experiences in school as a boy and gave me his philosophy on the art of instructing the young.

I tried again retiring to my own quarters, but found the kitchen filled with talking women preparing food. Since the bedroom was still full of babies, there was nothing for it but to return to the dance.

Around about midnight Mrs. Montgomery announced that lunch would be served and I felt like a besieged general when he sees relief coming over the hill. Big enamel pitchers of scalding coffee were brought up from the basement and served in thick, white kitchen cups. Chicken and pork sandwiches were passed around (there was virtually no market for chicken), followed by cake and cookies. I was waiting it out. Then each man rolled a fag or lighted up his pipe and the topic of economics was discussed in corners. Soon, I thought, even this will end. The kids will be cleared off my bed, everybody will go home and I'll get some sleep.

But I was greatly mistaken. Orville Jackson filled his pipe, hung it in place, and shuffled over to the organ again. Grandma Wilson draped her ample bottom over the organ stool. They struck up the music and the dance began again. And if I'd thought it lively before, now it was downright frantic. There was one slick little number where four men and four women joined hands. Then, with a quick manoeuvre, the men somehow had their arms behind the women's backs, hands clasped tight. They began to skip around in a circle, faster and faster. As the men gained momentum, the women's feet left the floor until their legs were straight out, their bodies parallel to the floor. I'd have sworn that if one had broken loose she'd have shot clear through the window.

Another feature of the after-supper session was what might be called the specialty numbers: dances performed by certain members who had become famous for them. "Dip and Dive", for instance, led by Uncle John Henry who weighed two seventy-five and was about five foot eight. Yet he had the grace and agility to lead the dancers, all holding hands, through an intricate series of dips and dives that was beautiful to watch. "Little Drops of Brandy" followed this, and a waltz quadrille.

But the specialty of specialties was when Orville Jackson and Grandma Wilson temporarily surrendered their instruments to an acne-afflicted youth and none other than our own Violet Sinclair. Then a reverent hush fell on the assembly as the two musicians took their places. Orville had set aside his peaked cap and pipe, revealing a head so bald and shiny that it gleamed beneath the gas lamp. As the music began the bald-headed man and the fat grandmother embraced each other for the only round dance of the evening. While the others formed a circle and clapped lightly and rhythmically to the tune of Till We Meet Again, those two danced as smoothly and gracefully as any couple I've ever seen.

And the dancing went on. One o'clock, two o'clock, three o'clock plodded by and there was no sign of a break. At six o'clock a faint glow of light began to show outside and the dancers reluctantly began to make preparations to leave. They had been waiting for daylight to make the long, long sleigh ride home just a little easier.

Sleeping babies, wound in their cocoons of blankets, were carried up the basement steps and laid gently in the straw in the bottoms of sleigh boxes. Horses with steam shooting from their nostrils were brought out from the barn and hitched to the sleighs. One by one they pulled out of the gate and I was left alone . . . alone with a schoolroom littered with cigarette and cigar butts, pipe ashes and tobacco juice. I thought it would never be clean again, but I was too tired to care.

I stumbled down the steps and into my bedroom, which smelled strongly of babies neglected for ten hours, peeled off my clothes and climbed beneath the covers. For half an hour the throbbing music still in my ears kept me awake, but then I sank into the deep sleep of the just.

Not for long. At nine o'clock I heard a heavy banging above me, feet on the stairs, my door being opened and somebody looking into the stove.

"It's only me," Mrs. Montgomery's voice announced cheerfully. "A few of us have come to clean up. We'll need to heat water on your stove. Some of that tobacco juice is hard to get off the floor." Then she added, "But you don't need to get up. I can find everything."

She thumped back up the stairs and, with four other ladies, tore into cleaning up the place. All morning they swept, scrubbed, scoured and, it seemed to me, played shuffleboard with the movable desks. Then, for good measure, they gave my kitchen-living room the same treatment and left.

Thus ended the one and only social event I attended during my stay at Willowgreen School.

7 Crime and punishment

I'd like to be able to report that there were no bad children in Willowgreen School. That these rugged, unspoiled country youngsters were all diamonds-in-the-rough – polite, respectful, hard-working, and co-operative. But that would be a lie. There was the usual quota of mean, nasty kids there. In fact, everywhere I've ever taught I've run into the same proportion of mean, nasty kids. They average about two to a classroom of thirty-five, which would be a little less than six per cent. And a little more than too many.

These are the brats who take every possible advantage of the teacher. They talk when his back is turned, make sly sotto voce comments on what he is saying, loaf, cheat, lie. Now, I know that there are supposed to be all sorts of reasons for this that lie deep in the child's id. That the kid isn't really naughty; just sick. I'm sorry, but to me they are still mean, nasty kids. That's all. They have no sense of decency or fairness and no respect for anybody. The only generalization I've been able to make is that mean, nasty kids usually come from mean, nasty parents. And I guess it's not hard to figure out where they came from.

How to handle them? An easy solution I've seen quoted in the papers, usually attributed to a judge, can be summed up in the advice... "Beat the stuffing out of them! Give them a taste of the strap. That will take the sneer off their faces." I don't agree. The idea of deliberately inflicting punishment has always been repugnant. Besides, violence begets violence. Each time a human is lashed with a cat-o-nine-tails, burned in an electric chair or has his neck broken by a rope, the whole race of man is degraded and civilization takes a step backwards.

But still, discipline is the biggest and least publicized of a teacher's problems.

The other day I heard a doctor remark that in six years of medical school, one in interning and three in post-graduate specialization, he'd never heard anyone mention the word "fee". "I never learned a thing about keeping books or collecting accounts," he said, "and as soon as I got into practice I discovered this to be my biggest concern."

Similarly with teachers' training. You learn about Pestalozzi, Abelard, John Dewey, and other great educators. You make endless charts, scrapbooks, nursery rhyme collections, and lesson plans. You fight with the intricacies of timetables. But the nasty word "discipline" is never mentioned. Then, when you enter a classroom, the very first thing that happens to you is one of those blasted six per centers.

And upon the way you handle him depends your whole success or failure as a teacher. Because nobody can teach anybody anything if he won't sit still and listen.

As an example of this I can cite two experiences I had some years later while supply teaching in Saskatoon. I went into a Grade Seven room in Princess Alexandra School where the children – the principal rather ashamedly informed me – were very democratic. I didn't know exactly what he meant until five minutes later when the class assembled, and then I learned he meant noisy, disrespectful, inconsiderate, and rude. They sauntered into the room, flopped into their seats, talked when I was talking, wandered about at will, and asked stupid questions. Before I could mark the register, I had to bang the desk bell three times to get their attention. Not only did they learn nothing, but they were restless, nervous, and insecure. After a week with them I'd developed a tic in my left cheek and my eyes had gone blurry.

Some weeks later I went to another room in the same school. (I didn't want to, but I needed the money.) Here the kids weren't at all "democratic". They stood quietly beside their desks when I entered and didn't sit until I asked them to. Then they remained quiet and still, but at the same time alert and inquisitive. Whereas in the other room I didn't dare begin a discussion for fear of it getting out of hand, here we had some good talks about literature, history, and current events. They learned something; I taught something. It was a pleasure to be there.

And that just about sums it up. Regardless of what a teacher thinks about discipline, the fact remains that if he doesn't have order in a class he's a goner. In high school we had a teacher called Williamson. Old Willie, we called him. He was intelligent, kind, reasonable and, as far as I know, a good husband and father. But he couldn't handle a roomful of adolescents. Every class was a shambles. We talked, threw chalk, stuck our feet into the aisle to trip each other, flicked paper wads with rulers, and made rude noises. The funny thing was, we had nothing against Old Willie, really. We'd just spotted a weakness and, being human, had to exploit it. A sore into which we had to rub salt. And, coldly and methodically with malice aforethought, we nice, normal kids ruined that man's career.

On the other hand, everybody can remember the tiny, fragile female teacher who kept perfect discipline.

What is this ability to keep discipline? Who knows. I do

know one thing, though, and that is that the thought of kids getting out of hand is a nightmare to most teachers. We have dreams about it. All the kids get out of hand and won't do a thing we say. Then we wake up in a cold sweat, glad that it isn't real. I wonder if financiers dream about the stock market going berserk on them.

But, whether a teacher is a "natural" disciplinarian or not, he must figure out some way of keeping on top of the class and handling the six per centers. I learned my first lesson by accident. On the very first day Bob Sanderson began to scuffle and I told him to remain after school. He did, sitting in his seat grinning widely as the others got their things on. But after they'd gone his grin faded a little. Since I hadn't a notion what to do with him, I stalled. Just left him there in his seat while I went on with some work.

I was really on the spot. I didn't know how to handle the situation. But I kept a stern mien and continued to ignore the culprit, hoping for some kind of inspiration.

As it turned out I didn't need it. The treatment I was giving him was the most effective possible – isolation and uncertainty. He was alone. Nobody to grin at, nobody to share his predicament. It's very easy for three children being punished together to feel that, at least by majority rules, they're more likely to be right than the teacher. But one child, all alone, is different from the others. He's been cut out; left the herd.

Gradually Bob's self-confidence and arrogance disintegrated. He felt terrible. And in direct proportion my own confidence and well-being increased. When he'd been there about three quarters of an hour and it came time when I had to do *something*, I continued to play it by ear and let him go without even a scolding. He left, still unsure. I never had any more trouble with him. In fact, we became good friends.

I've an idea that a juvenile caught committing his first theft or act of destruction might benefit from the same kind of treatment. Isolate him. Don't scold or threaten; children thrive on that. Just throw him into the coldest, dirtiest, miserablest jail cell available and leave him there, alone and without explanation. Let him sweat it out, think it over, become confused and frightened. Often the first mis-step is taken out of nothing more serious than boredom or devilment and, if the results are lonely, unpleasant, and unglamorous enough, if he's got any sense at all, he won't do it again.

Anyway, after years of teaching and more of being a parent I've formulated a few simple rules:

- Never punish two children together. You can get the other one next time.
- Never punish a class for the transgressions of a few. This is unfair and children have an overdeveloped sense of justice.
- Don't be too pally. This is particularly important if you go into the playground with the children. They'll immediately try – although they insist on fairness they are rarely fair themselves – to bring this free and easy relationship into the classroom. But you can't let it happen.
- Don't be afraid to get mad. I mean it. The saying about never striking a child in anger is the bunk. Rather, never strike a child *except* in anger. A good fast clout on the side of the head or a rap on the knuckles at the exact moment of the crime is worth ten lectures. It keeps them off balance. They don't know when it's going to come. Besides, because it's not cold-blooded or premeditated the children bear no grudges. They know they've aggravated you and made you mad. They also have a little fear of you in this mood, and a little fear is still the best deterrent to wrongdoing. Besides, it's easier on you. A teacher or parent who keeps complete control of himself

regardless of provocation is a teacher or parent with a stomach full of ulcers.

- The last rule is . . . don't permit yourself to be manoeuvred into a position where you'll have to do something drastic. In other words, avoid showdowns.

And this brings me to my disastrous showdown with Jake Stevenson.

Jake was a borderline six per center. That is, he grudgingly went along with the establishment in the classroom, but he made no bones about the fact that he didn't like it. In fact he treated the entire procedure and those responsible for it with complete contempt. Which is not surprising when you consider his parentage and way of life.

Leonard Stevenson, Jake's father, was a big, sandy-haired, sullen man fighting the battle for survival with no holds barred. He worked hard himself and expected everybody dependent upon him to work hard. He classed the weather, bad prices, mortgage companies and the government as enemies. Along with these he included the school. So far as he could see there was nothing taught there that was worth a tinker's damn to his kids. It didn't teach them how to plough, disc, seed or harvest. Therefore it was useless. But Leonard had learned that a lot of these useless things existed and honest, hard-working men were forced to support them. So, deep inside him glowed a sullen hatred of anything that didn't involve the land or the working of the land.

He'd inherited the land from his father, of the same name, who had homesteaded it in 1904, built the first sod hut on it, and worked like an ox to obtain clear title. No music, art, literature, or religion had played any part in his life. He'd worked hard, eaten immensely, rutted like a bull, and slept the sleep of the just. But, basically he was destructive. The land, his wife, and his children all suffered from his mining of the soil and his barrenness of soul. He was a destroyer.

Young Leonard was the same and Jake was no different. The third sullen Stevenson on the sullen land. At fourteen, Jake was as tall as I and weighed more. In his big horny hand a pencil looked like a garden rake being manipulated by a steam shovel. He didn't mind the arithmetic. It made sense, but to read a poem by Keats was to bring a look of bewildered contempt to his square, hard face.

Well, one day the inevitable happened. I turned around from writing a lengthy paragraph on the board and caught Jake with a double wrist lock on Charlie McDougall who sat behind him.

"All right, Jake," I said. "You'd better stay after school."

"Can't do that, Teacher. I've got to help my old man saw up some poplar poles."

"Just the same, you'll stay."

"And after that I've got to milk four cows and separate the milk."

All the other kids were watching this closely and I knew I'd have to make it stick. But the trouble was, of course, that Jake drove the Sinclair kids and the Friesens home with him, and if he stayed they'd have to walk or hang around and wait for him. I had manoeuvred myself right into a corner. Worst of all, Jake knew it. He sat with head low, watching me with cold, calculating eyes.

"You can take your choice, Jake. Either stay after school or get the strap."

This was the first time corporal punishment had even been mentioned, and the class stirred like a restless flock of sheep.

Jake's face went dark red, and he spoke slowly. "I'll take the licking."

A long, slow, collective sigh escaped from the throats of the others and they went back to work.

At recess time Jake stayed in his seat while the others cleared out. By now I was furious with him, not for what he'd done but for what he was making me do. I fished into the back of the desk drawer and brought out the piece of belting.

"All right, Jake. Come up here."

He came and I laid it on with all my strength. And, as I stood there pounding that boy's blistering hand, something very bad happened to me. I became a wild and savage being, wanting to hurt . . . hurt . . . hurt! Perhaps this is what happens to hangmen or torturers or even the Nazi guards at Buchenwald. A savage, fierce resentment builds up against the thing you are hurting because you are hurting it.

Jake made no movement and uttered no sound. But before I finished a small tear squeezed out from the corner of his eye and ran down between his cheek and nose. I turned away, but he knew I'd seen it. And I knew that proud, tough boy would never forgive me for seeing it.

He'd get back at me. I didn't know then how he'd manage it, but the next morning I found out.

When Jake entered the room he wasn't lugging the five-gallon cream can filled with water.

"Where's the water, Jake?" I asked.

"Not bringing it no more."

And that was that. I could make him stay in or lick him, but I couldn't force him to bring water. After school I walked over to see Dave McDougall; as secretary of the school district this was properly in his jurisdiction. He was in the yard making halter shanks out of binder twine. When I came up he neither stopped nor looked at me. For a moment I stood watching the long strands disappear into the small hand machine and be twisted into rope. Then I cleared my throat and said, "Jake Stevenson says he won't bring any more water to the school."

McDougall grunted and went on twisting twine.

I watched a while longer, trying not to let my aggravation show. "What will we do for water?"

He looked at me then. "You never should have licked that kid."

"But he deserved punishment."

"Maybe so. But the Stevensons are tough. They'll never supply no more water now."

"But I depend upon that water . . . to do my cooking . . . and everything."

He merely shrugged and went on twisting. And that was absolutely all I ever got out of him.

The next morning each child brought a small jar of water along with his lunch. And I had none. So, after school I walked the mile to Lyle English's place and got two pails of water from his well. Every second evening I took that long walk to fetch two pails of water. Nobody cared. Nobody ever said or did anything about it.

I never should have licked that kid!

8 The naked truth

It was several weeks after the dance that I welcomed the first visitor to my little home beneath the ground at Willowgreen. And this caller caught me in the most awkward of all conditions.

Saturday morning always presented me with a considerable personal problem: how to take a bath. To many of my constituents this was no problem at all. They simply stayed dirty. The old joke about the feller who said "I take a bath every twenty-fourth of May, whether I needs it or not," was literally true for many a prairie dweller in the grim thirties. Came the first cold weather in the fall, many climbed into their long woollen or fleece-lined underwear like a caterpillar crawling into a cocoon and didn't emerge until spring, even to sleep. Needless to say these suits took on a certain amount of body odour and it was best to stand down wind from the wearer. And when the heating system of the school was actually working, which was invariably on warm days, the air became so thick I'd throw open a window and stick my head out into the clean, frosty air to catch a breath of it.

In fact the whole question of cleanliness, about which we'd heard so much at Normal School, I completely omitted from my teaching. What point in telling these kids to wash their hands before they ate lunch when the one wash basin was full of holes and there was no water, except in the drinking fountain? And if they used that I'd have none.

Take a bath every day? What in, indeed, and with what water? Brush your teeth before retiring? These kids had no tooth brushes and had never tasted tooth paste. So, there were always one or two cases of impetigo or scabies (seven years' itch) along with plenty of bad teeth in the school. If cleanliness is really next to godliness this was the worst group of sinners west of Toronto.

I decided, however, that I would keep clean. Well, at least relatively clean. And so I dug out a round wash-tub from behind the furnace where it had been used to store old exam papers (I never did figure out why), cleaned it up and set it in the middle of my kitchen floor as near to the stove as I could get it.

Then I took all the pots and pans I had and went out to gather snow. There was plenty of that but none of it very clean. The strong winds that piled the snow in drifts tore the surface from the frozen fields and mixed it with the snow. However, where the wind whistled around the south-east corner of the building a fair drift had developed. By breaking through the thick crust I got my containers filled and carried them down the steps and set them on the stove. A heaping saucepan of snow gave me about a third of a saucepan of water, or a couple of cups. So it was up and down the steps with more snow. And since snow melts annoyingly slowly, even over a hot stove, it took all morning to get the tub one-quarter full of warm, gritty water. And by this time I really needed a bath.

To this day I never slosh about in a bathtub full of hot water or turn on a shower without a fleeting memory of those trips up and down the narrow basement stairway at Willowgreen.

On this particular morning I had got my tub half full, removed my clothes, stepped into the tub, sat down with my knees up under my chin, and begun to sing. It's the only place I do sing for the reason that it's the only place where I can be sure nobody will hear me. For, although I'm one of those rare persons who has no sense of pitch or key and who can't carry the simplest tune, I love to sing. I've heard my own voice on a tape recorder and know it to be flat, monotone, and raspy. But what I hear through the bones of my head when I'm splashing water around is the rich, mellow tenor of John McCormack. I don't stint either. I open my mouth wide and let her rip, so that I can be heard perfectly to the very back seats of Carnegie Hall.

Well, this morning I'd left the door into the other part of the basement wide open. Why not? There wasn't another living soul within a mile. I was just ripping into the best part of "That Little Grey Shack in Athlone" where I really hit it big, when a long hooked nose poked around the door frame, followed by the scruffy countenance of Harris Montgomery.

I stopped in mid-note and stared.

His black eyes were big with wonder. "Why, that's really nice," he said.

Like all artists I'm extremely susceptible to praise. "Do you really think so?" I started to get up.

"No, no, no, don't get up," he urged. "Go right ahead. Surely to God there's no need for petty bourgeois false modesty here."

"Huh?"

"Besides, I know how hard it is to get warm water for a bath and keep it that way. Go ahead, go ahead. I'll just sit here." Without removing his peaked cap or his mackinaw he sat down on my kitchen chair, pushed back some dishes, and leaned his elbow on the edge of my dirty table.

From my vantage point in the tub I peered around at

the mess of clothing, utensils, and papers on my floor and felt like a housewife caught unawares. "If I'd known you were coming, I'd have swept the floor," I quipped.

The hawk eyes glared and the hawk beak quivered. "Too damned much sweeping and scrubbing goes on in the world anyway," he barked. "My wife. My God! Every time you look at her she's got a broom in her hand or a mop. 'What's the use of all that sweeping and cleaning?' I ask her. 'Just because your mother did it and her mother and hers. I tell you things have changed. We've got to strip ourselves of all those old ideas. All of them. Got to start new in every way.' "

"What does she say to that?"

"Her? Hah! Tells me to save my speeches for the political meetings. That's the trouble. Nobody's thinking. Why do you suppose we're getting forty-three cents a bushel for our wheat? Why?"

"Because your wife sweeps the floor?"

"That's part of it. Yes it is. Part of the cloudy, irrepressible thinking of the day. Ineptitude to throw off the old yokes. We've got nothing to lose but our chains."

I asked him if he'd mind getting me the cake of soap which had squirted out of my hand into the corner.

He did without missing a word. "What do you think is the cause of these hard times anyway? What do you think it is? Come on, tell me."

"Well . . . uh . . . a lot of things, I guess."

"No, dammit no. One thing. How much money you got?"

"None."

"See, what did I tell you? What did I tell you, man?" He jabbed the air with his hands to make his point and nodded his head violently.

"You mean it's the lack of money?" I asked.

"What else, man?" He leaped from his chair and almost into the tub with me. "The insurance companies and the banks and other vested interests has got it all. Every bit of it. And you know why?" He was standing over me now, bent almost double, his face close to mine. "I'll tell you why. The profit motive. That's why. Mark my words. Production for profit instead of production for use!" Having delivered his bomb he sat down on the chair and crossed his legs again, staring at me intently.

"Uh yes, I guess that's so," I said, trying to reach around to my back with the wash cloth.

Without a word he took the cloth from my hand and began to scrub my back. "We've solved the production problem," he said in time to the scrubbing. "Why look, man!" He straightened up and the soapy water dripped on the floor. "I heard on the radio last night where down in California they're piling potatoes into a pit, pouring gasoline on them, and setting fire to the whole thing. Just to get rid of them! And there's people need those spuds. Starving for them! Literally starving!" He waved the cloth and soapy water spattered the walls. "Doesn't that prove we've solved the problem of production? Doesn't it?"

His face was close to mine again.

"Yes, I suppose it does."

"Of course it does. Of course. And it's the same with everything else. Look at these combines they're bringing out for the western farmer. Cut and thresh a whole crop in no time with two men. Two men. Why, I mind when a threshing outfit would have twenty men! Twenty! And manufacturing. Mass production. Assembly lines. Turn out hundreds of cars a day! Hundreds! You see what I mean, don't you?"

"Yes, I . . . think so. . . ."

"Well, what's the answer, eh? What? I'll tell you what. We've got to solve the means of distribution, so that all these things that are being made can be distributed to the people who need them. And what stands in the way of that? Money. Or the fact that nobody's got any. Aberhart over in Alberta.

He's trying to do something about it. Ever listen to him on the radio?"

"No. I uh . . . don't have a radio."

"Too bad. Why, that man's talking sense. Give people the money, he says. Twenty-five dollars a month to every man, woman, and child."

"Without earning it?"

"Don't you see? He earns it by being a consumer. You pay a man for consuming. So he buys things. Buys things to keep the wheels of industry turning." He dropped the wash cloth into my lap. "I've got to be going. Supposed to be over at McDougall's getting a meat grinder. Thought I'd drop in on you since you're so interested in Cole. Brought you a couple of books. One by Major C. H. Douglas. He's the British economist Aberhart keeps talking about. Another by G. D. H. Cole. *A Guide Through World Chaos*. We've got chaos right enough. Read them. Just read them and see what you think." He went out the door and up the steps.

Thus, sitting in four inches of tepid, murky snow water, did I receive my first lesson in prairie socialism. But it was not to be my last. Harris Montgomery was typical of many farmers I met while teaching in Saskatchewan during the early thirties. Bewildered, embittered men they were, who had fought drought, grasshoppers, gophers, blizzards, frost, and heaven knows what else to establish homes on the plains. Mostly they were uneducated men who'd come west instead of going to school. Prior to the war they'd seen good times and bad, but mainly their fight was against nature. After the war times had been good. And now, because of a mysterious force called "economics" about which they knew nothing, they were losing everything and they began to ask themselves "Why?" Why is a bushel of wheat worth two dollars ten years ago now worth forty cents? Same wheat. Same sweat and work and worry goes into producing it. Why? Why? Why?

And this led them into the labyrinth of economic theory:

supply and demand, profit and loss, foreign trade, fiscal policies. In the long winter nights by flickering coal-oil lamps men who for years hadn't read anything more than the *Free Press Prairie Farmer* pored over books they didn't understand, often mouthing the unfamiliar phrases again and again, memorizing them, running their fingers along the lines to keep the place. They kept dictionaries by their sides, looked up the words of the economic jargon, and fitted them into their conversation, often with devastating results. They wore out their eyes studying and sent to Eaton's for glasses. Such were the early prairie socialists, born out of a desperate need to save themselves from destruction by a foe they couldn't see or understand.

Later other educated and trained men were to enter the field and lead new political parties, but the ones I remember best were the mavericks, the pioneers in the movement. The ones with the fire in their eyes.

I was thinking of Harris Montgomery's words as I lugged dirty bathwater by the panful up the steps. Then the front door of the school burst open and he was there again, stamping and blowing and waving his arms.

"The schoolhouse!" he shouted.

"Huh?" I set the pan of water down and stared at him.

"We could have a meeting here. The idea struck me on the way back from McDougall's. I could get Dan Trowbridge to come over from Kindersley. Now there's a man who really knows how to run a meeting."

"What kind of a meeting?"

"A political meeting. For the new socialist party that's being formed. You've heard of it, haven't you?"

"Well . . . vaguely. There was some sort of meeting in Calgary."

His head jerked like a turkey's. "Last August. The founding meeting. Dan Trowbridge was there. I tell you the new party's going to sweep this province."

"But a provincial election's not until next year!"

"I know, I know, I know. But we've got a lot of education work to do. Got to have an informed electorate. Up until now people been voting in a Liberal government – except for this last Conservative one – because that's the way they've always voted, and because they might get a road job out of it or something. No informed voting. We got to teach the people that in a real democracy the voter must think! Think!" He held his fist on high.

"When would you want to have this meeting?"

Without hesitation he burst out. "Two weeks from today. In the afternoon. Yes. That will give us time to work up some interest in the community. Get the people out. If we can get them out we can convince them." He looked at me with narrowed, calculating eyes. "How about you?"

"I'll be here. Nowhere else to go."

"As a speaker, I mean. Yes, by the peel-heeled Johnny Morgan, that's the ticket. A new voice. The voice of youth, deprived of its rightful place, forced to teach school for a starvation wage in a poorly equipped school. Yes sir. And you can speak also for all these young men who are riding the rods from place to place. No jobs. No hope. Just a trainman's boot up their bottom or a Mountie's club on the head. Living in hobo jungles, starving in this land of plenty!"

"But I've never ridden the rods."

"No, but many a young man your age is riding them right now. Isn't that a fact?'

It was indeed. Thousands of them riding in boxcars west to Vancouver looking for work and, finding none, riding back again. I thought of the schoolmate who, being inexperienced at ride stealing, had stayed on top of a boxcar when the train went through a tunnel in the Rockies, was overcome by the smoke and ashes from the engine and fell beneath the wheels. He'd wanted me to go with him, and if this teaching job hadn't turned up I undoubtedly would have.

And I thought of my annual $450 salary and my wretched living conditions and the kids deprived of a decent education. Suddenly I too was very angry. "All right," I said. "I'll make a speech."

"Good, good, good. I'll write to Dan Trowbridge right away. There's a lot of organization work to to. A lot. Well, I better be going. I'll let you know the details."

Thus did I enter into my one, brief scuffle with politics and became acquainted with the leaders and the led and those who just don't give a damn. It was as disastrous as it was brief.

First off I learned that politics is one of those activities that no "real" teacher will become involved with. Too dirty, too crooked. Better keep out of it. On the Wednesday evening after Harris Montgomery's visit I suddenly found my place unbearable. I had to get out. So I did what I always did when the limit of endurance had been reached. Grabbed my coat and hat and ran up the stairs as though the furies were after me – which they were – and headed across the field to Lyle English's place.

Mrs. English let me in the back door. To this day I'm not sure whether she liked me or not, whether these unannounced visits of mine were a pleasing break in the week's monotony or a bloody nuisance. She rarely smiled or commented, but simply put up with me. Now, however, she appeared strangely animated. "Well, well, if it isn't our budding politician," she exclaimed, smiling conspiratorially. "Come in, come in."

I grinned stupidly. "Budding what?"

"Aren't you going to speak to the rattleheads?"

"The what?"

"Oh. Uh . . . that's a name some people call the people who are . . . uh . . . always talking about changing everything. You know . . . radicals."

"That's interesting. Perhaps things need changing . . . a little."

"Oh dear, I don't know anything about politics. You'll have to discuss that with Lyle." She said this as one might say, "You'll get it all straightened out when you get in the ring with Jack Dempsey."

When Lyle finally finished his chores, washed his hands at the wash basin in the kitchen and came into the living room, he didn't beat around the strawstack.

"What's this about you speaking at the communist meeting?" he asked.

"The what?"

"Old Harris Montgomery, the great freethinker and non-worker, is telling around the district that you're going to speak."

"But he said it was an education meeting . . . sort of a discussion group for the new party."

He laughed. "You mean the Communists."

"I understood they were Socialists."

"Call them what you want, they're still Communists. Listen, all we need to do is throw out that Anderson Government and put the Liberals back in power. Biggest mistake this province ever made, voting in those Conservatives."

I was over my depth already. Like most young people, my interest in politics had been pretty well confined to arguments in high school. Each election all the children whose fathers were Conservative would pitch into all those whose fathers were Liberal. My dad being a John A. Macdonald Conservative, I was always on the minority and losing side.

Now I was being challenged to do some thinking.

"Uh . . . what about . . . uh . . . poverty in the midst of plenty?" I countered.

This time his laugh was a roar. "By God I see you've been picking up some of that old nut's catch phrases. But let me tell you, if he'd stay home and do some farming instead of leaving it all to his wife and son Les, he wouldn't be so damned poor."

"But what good will work do when the prices are so bad? I mean . . . uh . . . the vested interests control everything anyway, no matter which of the old-line parties is in power."

He didn't laugh this time. "Look here, I know things aren't perfect. I've got a loan at the bank, too, that I'm having trouble paying. But that's due to the drought and the bad price for wheat. Good God, let's not burn down the barn because the manure pile's too big. These crackpots talk about socialism. They want to take everything from everybody and spread it all around! That's fine for them. They've got nothing anyway. I tell you, when we get the Liberals back in power... both in Saskatchewan and Ottawa . . . things will change. I've worked hard for my farm. And I own it clear. I'm not going to give it up to those crackpots!"

"But . . ."

"Take this idea of theirs about socializing the banks and setting up a central bank. What good would that do? Did you ever see anything run by politicians that wasn't either crooked or stupid?"

"But don't you think unemployment insurance, for instance, might be a good thing?"

"Unemployment insurance! Are you crazy? Paying a man for not working! Who's going to work if he can get paid for not working? Answer me that! It's against human nature. And this damned fool over in Alberta, promising everybody twenty-five dollars a month for nothing. Did you ever hear anything so crazy in your life?"

That I didn't fully appreciate the wisdom of his words can only be attributed to my youth and inexperience. I hung doggedly on. "What about a minimum wage? Don't you think that would be good?"

"Does the farmer get a minimum wage? In a pig's eye he

does. He gets what he can earn by the sweat of his brow. If prices are down the way they are now, how's he going to pay his help a minimum wage? Well, how?"

I didn't know. It has always been one of my less admirable characteristics that a forceful spokesman can convince me of anything. I'd been convinced by Harris Montgomery and now I was being convinced by Lyle English. And I was supposed to speak at a meeting.

Then Lyle English resolved my dilemma by saying one thing too many. "Besides," he leaned over, lowered his voice and tapped me on the knee with a horny forefinger. "Folks in the district aren't going to take kindly to the teacher speaking at a socialist meeting. They might not take you on for another term."

Take me on for another term! At four hundred and fifty lousy dollars a year! For this I was to give up my right to say what I wanted to when I wanted to? Since the smells from the kitchen promised a better meal than I'd had in weeks, I restrained myself from teeing off on my unctious host. But I decided to speak at that meeting.

Right here I'd like to be able to report that the schoolhouse was packed with sceptical people that day, that I convinced them by the sheer power of my oratory, had been chosen candidate for the district, and had gone on to lead these poor serfs from the wilderness. But nothing like that happened at all. My guts were so badly chewed up with loneliness, frustration, and natural, twenty-year-old urges that I never got around to actually preparing a speech. But I wasn't concerned. After all, I'd only be speaking to a bunch of stupid farmers. I made a few mental notes that sounded pretty good and let it go at that.

Came the afternoon of the meeting. (I'll try to give as accurate a picture as possible, because these early schoolhouse educational gatherings were unique in Canadian politics.) Around two in the afternoon farmers, some with wives and children, began to arrive on horseback, in sleighs, and on foot. By three all the benches, made by laying planks from seat to seat, were packed. People were even standing at the back.

Dan Trowbridge was there, having come to Alsask from Saskatoon by train and been picked up there by young Tom Thurston who owned the fastest team of drivers in the district. And, after the meeting, Tom would drive him back again to catch the train east. A round trip of close to fifty miles in an open cutter to speak to fewer than fifty farmers.

Trowbridge was completely unlike any idea I had of a political organizer. Here was none of the derby hat, velvet collar, and swaggering gait. Instead, a slim young man of about twenty-five in a conservative suit. A recent graduate of the University of Saskatchewan in political science, he'd thrown himself wholeheartedly into the new movement. Only his intelligent flashing eyes gave an indication of the fire that burned inside. With him he'd brought Sheila Barnes, a girl of about his own age, dark, trim, and stylish with a broad, generous smile.

As Harris Montgomery opened the meeting and mouthed his favourite clichés, Trowbridge and Sheila Barnes sat on straight chairs beside my desk, calmly sizing up their audience. It was as hard-headed a group as you'd want to see, about two-thirds Liberals and one-third Conservatives. All capitalists to the core, being owners of land and machinery, and employers of labour. All sceptical of anyone in a city suit or a well-cut dress with a swishy skirt. Grim-faced, disillusioned, cantankerous, they sat, saying by their looks and manner: "All right, you young whippersnappers, show me."

Well, Dan Trowbridge and Sheila Barnes showed them all right. After his introduction, Dan got up and said he felt like the man who was asked how he felt about being tarred and feathered and ridden out of town on a rail. "If it weren't for the honour, I'd just as soon have walked," the man said. A few in the audience smiled appreciatively.

Then Dan introduced his partner and, much to everybody's surprise, she went over to the organ, sat on the stool, placed her hands on the chipped old keys, and drew forth sweeter music than anyone had heard from it. Then Dan Trowbridge took his place by the desk and sang "Shortening Bread" in a passable tenor voice. And ever since, when I hear that song sung by anyone, I see that slim young man at the front of my schoolhouse. After the surprised applause Sheila sang "Danny Boy" to her own accompaniment, and this time the applause was longer and louder.

Then the two of them did a little skit which I can't remember much about now except that it involved a farmer and his wife and their problems with dust, drought, and Russian thistle. It must have been funny because the audience roared. Then Dan told a few jokes like the one about the farmers who were being shown through the insane asylum in Battleford. They sadly watched an inmate doggedly going through the elaborate motions of pitching a baseball, and, when the delegation moved on, one stayed behind. When asked why, he replied, "I was studying his style. Another year like the last one and I'll be in here catching for him."

After that, with his audience properly softened up, this remarkably talented man gave a clear, reasonable explanation of the social democratic state, drawing heavily on Sweden for comparisons.

At least that's what I think he did. For, to tell the truth, I wasn't listening. I was on fire. As a student at Nutana Collegiate and later at the Normal School, dramatics had been my forte. Another fellow and I wrote and acted in a series of skits that were, in their small way, famous in the school. And now the thrill of performing came back to me with an excitement so great that it drove from my mind all thoughts of the speech I was scheduled to give.

After Dan Trowbridge had finished speaking and had disposed of the questions from the audience in a neat and informed manner, Harris Montgomery got up and introduced me. "And now we're going to hear from a brilliant young man who finds himself caught in the toils of this wretched state of affairs. He will talk about the point of view of youth."

My God!

It has been my fate through the years that just when I particularly need to be good I'm terribly bad. Given a mediocre situation where nothing is at stake and I can be brilliant. Let the occasion be momentous and the stakes high and I lay an egg. The one I laid on this occasion would have made an omelet to feed that whole yawning crowd. What ideas had been in my head left when I faced those sceptical farmers and their wives. I mumbled a few clichés that would have made Harris Montgomery blush and sat down. All the following week, of course, I was tortured with thoughts of the brilliant phrases, witty sarcasm, fine irony, learned satire, and comedy that raced through my mind night and day.

At the conclusion of the meeting, while the ladies were serving lunch, I sought out Dan and Sheila and tried to engage them in conversation. But they weren't much interested. To them I was just another dull schoolteacher.

And as I watched them drive away in the cutter drawn by two prancing horses, I had a stone in my heart. God, how I wanted to go with them! To be part of this exciting, vibrant thing they were doing.

What did I care if they were right or wrong? Socialism shmocialism! And what if they did drive fifty miles in a cutter in sub-zero weather? They had each other to keep warm. They were the new spirit of the West, pioneers like their fathers, doers, fighters, crusaders.

I went down into my miserable digs and cursed myself for an hour by the clock.

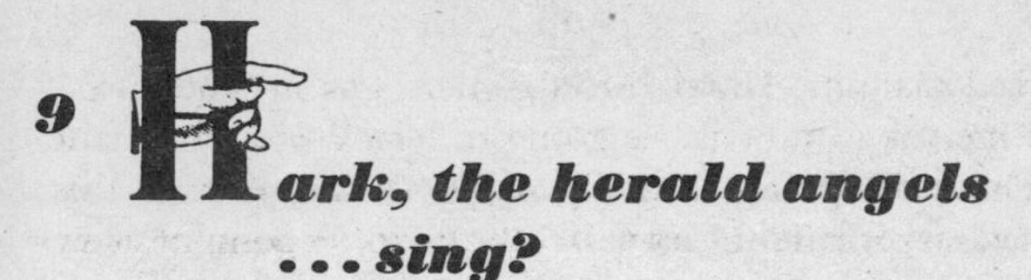

9 Hark, the herald angels ... sing?

At this point, with the reader's indulgence, I will interrupt the smooth, even flow of the Willowgreen saga to talk about Christmas concerts. And I hope this will end the subject once and for all.

Although not specifically spelled out in the course of studies, in the prairie rural school of the dirty thirties the Christmas concert was far and away the most important event of the year. It involved everyone in the district, from the oldest grandmother to babes in arms.

But most of all it involved the teacher. In fact, to a large extent he was judged by his ability to put on a good concert. He might let the children run over him, neglect their reading, get muddled in math, make a bad call against the local team while umpiring ladies' softball, or even fail to court the chairman's daughter, and get away with it. But let him fail to stage "the best concert we've had yet," and he was dead.

It was in my next school after Willowgreen that I staged my most memorable concert. Memorable? Chaotic is a better word. In fact, it is the only word. The memory of it lies in my mind like rock in a sack, and I still squirm like a worm on a hook when I hear "Hark, the Herald Angels."

Compared to Willowgreen, this school which I shall call Haldane was in the heart of civilization. Not more than five miles away was a hamlet of seventy-one persons with all the amenities such a community affords. Haldane was built on the same general plan as Willowgreen – most prairie schools of that era were – except that the district had run out of money before installing chemical toilets in the basement. So, the facilities were outside about fifty yards from the schoolhouse, up against the fence. Also, I didn't live in this school but boarded with a farmer about a mile down the road. These facts are essential to the story or I wouldn't mention them.

Anyway, early in November I began training my twenty-eight children for the concert. An irrevocable rule of this institution is that every child, regardless of ability, sex, size, or inclination, must be given exactly as much to do in the concert as every other child. Parents, grandparents, uncles, aunts, godparents and friends insisted that this rule be observed. They drove to the school in below-zero weather to see their favourites perform and would brook no partiality by any smart-alec schoolteacher.

If memory serves me right, we had no less than thirty items in this concert, consisting of recitations, sketches, solos, pageants, plays, skits, pantomimes, dances, drills, monologues, magic acts, Santa Claus, and choruses. Oh Lord . . . those choruses!

A very few times in each generation the fates, in a sardonic mood, so muddle up the genes in an individual that he is born completely without a sense of music. I don't mean he isn't a good singer. He's no singer. He can't even whistle or hum a tune. It's the opposite to perfect pitch. It's nothing pitch.

Such a one am I.

I consider anybody who can pick out any kind of a tune

on anything a genius. My mind becomes a dead thing when confronted with those little black dots with stems on them that other people see as notes representing sounds. At the Normal School the music teacher, a Madame Perry who enjoyed a considerable local reputation as a singer, once asked me to teach a song by rote. I still don't know what this could possibly mean, except that it is different from "by note", which also baffles me. I went up to the front of the room, scratched my seat, drew five lines on the blackboard, turned and looked at her with such suffering that she told me to sit down.

She already knew about me. Like every other music teacher I'd had in every grade, she'd listened to me try to sing a note once and then told me henceforth to shut up.

Well, at least fifty per cent of any Christmas concert is music. I kept away from it as long as possible, concentrating on skits, recitations, and the rest, but finally I had to face up to it.

"Can anybody play the organ?" I asked the class.

A hand from a seat near the back went up. It belonged to Marjorie Quick who was freckle-faced, snub-nosed, and in Grade Nine.

"Good," I said. "We'll begin practising our Christmas carols. What can you play, Marjorie?"

Marjorie shrugged and slouched over to the organ and began to play "Hark the Herald Angels". At least it sounded like that, but there was something wrong, too. It didn't sound exactly right. I hesitantly suggested this to Marjorie . . . people with nothing pitch are pretty deferential about such things . . . and she swivelled on the stool and asked, "How does it go then?"

This was like asking a Zulu tribesman how to knot an ascot tie. Marjorie played completely by ear and had I been able to hum the tune all would have been well. As it was she had to go with what she had.

So we practised this with the kids singing as loudly as they could. Then we did "Jingle Bells" and "King Whats-his-name" and several others. They all sounded all right to me. But the angels. Somehow there was something wrong.

As we approached the Friday before Christmas, the traditional date for concerts, the school time was given over completely to practices. Besides, there were a thousand details to be arranged, not the least of which was the finding of a Santa Claus.

I solved this by making a deal with a friend who was principal of the continuation school in the town. I'd be his jolly man and he'd be mine. Now the playing of Santa Claus at school concerts follows a set, unchangeable pattern. The suit is red and scruffy, the boots rubber and high, the beard a wispy bit of white cotton dangling from the chin. The general demeanour is rather diffident and quiet, the whole idea being to try and prevent all the children from figuring out in the first few seconds which local personage lurks behind the beard. They'll catch on soon enough, but these first few seconds seem important.

Well, I decided that this wasn't good enough. There should be some life, some sparkle, some humour in the old boy. And that cotton beard wouldn't do at all. So I cast about for a better one. It turned out there was none in the district, but when I'd been visiting the farm of Sam Melville, who kept sheep, I'd seen the hide of a ram thrown over a fence. The very thing.

I cut off a piece of this hide, combed the wild oats and dust out of it, made a hole for my mouth near the top and shaped a passable moustache and beard. But I didn't do anything to remove the smell, and this oversight later almost cost me my life.

Came the evening of my friend's concert. The town hall was packed with every man, woman, and child from a radius of ten miles, and the place was hot as an outdoor phone booth in July.

I waited outside the door, observed and sniffed by a couple of dogs who had never before encountered such a Santa Claus. Then the fake telegrams had all been read, and I was on. With a ringing of bells and a great deal of ho-ho-hoing, I bounded down the aisle and onto the stage.

"Helllllo boys and girls!" I roared.

Dead silence.

Then back with my head and out with a blast of lusty ho-ho-ho's.

More silence.

So I pranced up and down the stage, clicked my heels and bellowed about how cold it was at the North Pole.

Nothing.

I still had a bag of tricks. I'd composed a monologue filled with terribly funny comments about local residents and some jokes left over from my Nutana Collegiate triumphs. As I delivered these in my most comical manner I noted a certain restlessness in my audience, but no laughter.

And I was quickly becoming aware of another problem that transcended my poor reception. The heat of the building plus that of my blushing countenance had got to the uncured hide of Melville's ram, and it was beginning to stink. Now a beard, by its very nature, must be worn in close proximity to the nose and, in fact, I had to breathe through it in order to survive.

This, along with the fact that I'd dropped my paper of witty sayings and the rope I was using for a belt had come untied, made me lose some of my earlier enthusiasm for my skit. Dance and jollity and jokes all came to a grinding stop in the middle of the stage, and I called upon my elves – some teachers and Sunday School leaders standing self-consciously by – to distribute the goodies from under the tree. I got the hell out of there. Never did fresh air smell so good.

But to get back to my own concert. A week before opening night a half dozen farmers moved in, fetched planks from the basement, and laid them on sawhorses to make a narrow stage across the front of the room. Then they shoved most of the desks back against the wall and laid planks over the others to make benches. The old school had become a theatre.

The next five days were solid rehearsals. And not one child, not one of the entire twenty-eight knew more than a couple of words of what he was to say. But I had standards. This thing of a prompter behind the curtain hissing louder than the performers wasn't good enough. So, I drilled and shouted and paced up and down between the benches clutching at my forehead. And they looked at me with watery eyes wondering why all the fuss. They'd been in lots of concerts. They knew how things would be. But this was my first time.

The night of the concert came and with it the worst blizzard of the year. The wind velocity increased all day, and by six o'clock it was a real snorter.

"Well," I said, pressing my nose against the frosty window pane and noting the swirling snow, "I guess nobody'll venture out on a night like this."

"Get away with you," my landlady scoffed. "A little snow like this won't keep folks away from the Christmas concert!"

She was an ex-schoolteacher and I had a bad feeling she knew what she was talking about.

She and I and her husband, all the presents and candy for under the tree, plus assorted bits of costume, a wooden telephone for a skit, and a couple of recently completed shepherd's crooks were all to be picked up by Alvin Carmen and his family who would arrive at seven via a trail across the field. Seven o'clock went by, and eight and eight-thirty. No Carmens. Outside the storm got steadily worse.

Then, about nine o'clock we heard a noise in the yard, and in a moment Alvin Carmen appeared at the back door looking like a snowman. There was snow in his eyebrows, eyelashes, and moustache. "Come on," he puffed. "We'll be late for the concert."

"What happened?"

"Got lost in the field. Kept going round in circles. Never would have got straightened out if Tommy hadn't noticed a frozen rabbit we'd passed twice before." Then he added philosophically, "Worst night I've ever been out in."

Nothing, I'm sure, could have brought anyone out that night except a Christmas concert.

So we loaded the stuff into the sleigh box where Mrs. Carmen and the three kids were huddled down in the straw. The road from there to the school was straight and between fences. So, we made it without trouble. To my surprise the school yard was full of rigs, the barn full of horses, and the school full of people. They filled every inch of planking and stood at the back and along the sides. And still they came. Each time the door opened, snow blew half way across the room. Inside, the air was thicker than soup. Above, the gas lamp sputtered and hissed. The tiny candles on the tree tilted crazily. If fire had broken out there, sixty people would have perished without a chance. But they never even gave that a passing thought. It was the Christmas concert.

In the cramped space behind the curtain I went crazy with costumes, make-up, and props. It wasn't easy to keep my huge cast under control. The little girls primped, swished about, giggled, and posed. The boys grinned, poked each other, shoved, and wrestled. All of them were so hopped up with excitement that they'd forgotten everything they were to say or do.

There was a commotion in the audience. A large woman, packed in against the window on the side of the room furthest from the door, lifted a two-year-old child from her lap and passed it over her head to the man behind. Without a word, he took it and passed it into the outstretched hands of the woman behind him. So, like a medicine ball, the child was passed from hand to hand over the heads of the audience to a man leaning against the door jamb who took it outside for what had to be done. Back inside again, the child was passed over the heads to the mother. She plunked it onto her knee, gave it a little jiggle and looked sternly towards the stage.

We were ready to begin. Marjorie Quick, who alone of all the cast had kept calm, struck a chord on the organ and the audience struggled to its feet for "God Save The King." Then the chairman of the board in blue serge suit came onto the stage and counted it a pleasure and a privilege to thank each and every one who had contributed to making this concert the great success he was sure it was going to be. Then he added that, for him, the best part of any Christmas concert was hearing those eager young voices singing those . . . "dear old Christmas carols we remember so well from our childhood."

I didn't pay much attention, because I had other problems, not the least of which was the absence of my friend who was to be Santa Claus. Nobody but a fool could be expected to go out to somebody else's concert on a night like that, and he was no fool. This meant another session with the fleece of Melville's ram.

I shoved the first child onto the stage, a six-year-old who recited a thing about being just a little boy who hadn't much to say except to wish them a happy Christmas day. He remembered two-thirds of it and drew prolonged applause from the corner of the house where his relatives predominated.

Then the entire ensemble wiggled and giggled its way on stage and sang "Jingle Bells". So far, so good. More recitations, some skits, an action song, a drill, and we were ready for "Hark the Herald Angels". I could have used a couple of those angels myself – guardian type.

Marjorie struck a chord. The children opened their mouths. From behind the curtain I peeked at the audience. As the singing began a most unusual expression spread over their collective faces. A combination of wonderment, horror, disbelief, and a sort of over-all sadness at the terrible things that can happen to people in this world.

There was no applause at the end, just stunned silence. I was completely baffled at this and quite hurt. It wasn't until I got home for the holiday and heard "Hark the Herald Angels" come over the radio that I understood their reaction. The two tunes had nothing in common.

And to this day, when the joyous season is upon us and the air is filled with carols, I get up and quietly leave the room where the radio is playing. My kids look after me and wonder what's wrong, for I've never told them what happened. The memory of "Hark the Herald Angels" is far too painful, altogether.

10  Lady in the snow

The trouble with looking backward is that from the closet of memory you drag forth skeletons that might better be left in peace. So it is with Alice Field. Perhaps I should leave her out of this, but her story is so much a part of the story of the plains in the years after the first World War, when thousands of British war brides were led there like lambs into the wilderness, that it must be told. Besides, it is a tender memory.

It happened during a blizzard. In my experience there is nothing meaner, crueler, and more relentless than a prairie blizzard. People who live in the kinder climates of the East often make silly remarks like, "I know it's cold on the prairies, but it's a dry cold and you don't really notice it." This is like saying, "So you fell a hundred feet off a tower. You landed on clay. Be a lot worse if you'd landed on concrete." Either way, you're dead.

When the temperature is twenty-five below and a fifty-mile-an-hour wind comes screeching out of the northwest, no man can stand against it. Farmers have got lost and frozen to death going from house to barn. The winds swirling about your head deprive you of all sense of direction. Eyelids freeze shut, lungs ache, faces turn a dirty, livid white with frost-bite. No one in his right mind goes out in a blizzard.

This one began in the early hours of a Friday morning. I was awakened by the high whine made by a loose piece of siding, where some child had hit it with a baseball bat. A sure sign the wind had reached a velocity of more than fifty miles an hour.

I was up before daylight to stoke up my fire and, after eating, went up to the schoolroom and looked out the window. The wind hadn't reached its full force. I could still see the barn, but beyond that was a grey mass of swirling snow. No children would show up today, I knew, because this had the look of a two- or three-day blow. There was enough water in the cooler to last a couple of days, if I didn't wash, but the prospect of being with myself for that long made me sick at the stomach.

Then I saw a muffled figure on a shaggy horse coming out of that wall of snow like an apparition coming through a mist. I shook my head in disbelief. It was there all right. He slid from the horse, pushed the barn door open and led the horse inside.

I waited, five minutes, ten minutes, but nobody came out. So I got into my coat and rubbers and fought my way to the barn. It was a bare, empty place, cold and clammy. The horse was tied in the stall, and sitting on a tiny mound of straw that somebody had put there for bedding was a woman, bundled up in a mackinaw and toque.

"Why . . . it's, it's Mrs Field," I blurted, which wasn't as foolish a remark as it sounds, because, to tell the truth, she looked so strange I hardly recognized her. Wide-eyed, staring, as though she were in shock. My next question was perhaps sillier than the first. "What are you doing here?"

She looked at me then, with large, dark eyes in a white face. "I've left."

"Left home? But why?"

She stared straight ahead without answering, and I knew she wasn't going to answer. "Come, you can't stay here. You'll freeze." I took her by the thin shoulders and raised her to her feet. The barn door stuck with the snow piling against it, but I managed to shove it open. The wind was stronger than ever now, and the schoolhouse scarcely visible. I wrestled the door shut and hooked it, and together we struggled through the snow to the school.

When I got her inside the door she was shaken with long spasms of shuddering and violent coughing. "Downstairs," I said. "There's a good fire there."

In the warmth of my kitchen the shudders became less frequent. She took off her outer clothing. Underneath the sheepskin mackinaw she wore a sweater and underneath that a neat cotton dress. And underneath the dress she had pulled on a pair of heavy khaki trousers that must have been part of her husband's army uniform. The seat bagged out at the back under her cotton dress, like a bustle.

She sat down on one of my two kitchen chairs, stared at me for a second, then buried her face in her hands and cried like a little child. Even now, having been married for years and having raised three daughters, I still don't know what to do when a female cries. At twenty, shy and naturally awkward in the presence of women, I was completely baffled. I stood up, advanced with my right hand extended tentatively, and touched her shoulder. I'll swear the flesh quivered and something very natural happened to me . . . a strong urge to take her in my arms and comfort her in the only way that a man can comfort a woman.

But I didn't. No, I went out the door like a shot and up the stairs. Then I paced back and forth in front of the windows. What to do. Here I was with a woman on my hands. Not an old woman, either. The storm had reached its full force and might stay that way for a couple of days. I had no phone, no horse and sleigh. Her husband, I recalled vaguely from the dance, was a big, raw-boned, loud-voiced man, lean and powerful. The last place he would look for his wife, providing he dared venture out at all, would be at the schoolhouse.

Why was she here? Had she really left home?

When I went back downstairs, Mrs. Field had taken off the khaki trousers, combed her hair and was nervously tidying up my room.

"My goodness but things are in a mess here," she said. "Just like a man, don't know the first thing about keeping a house clean. My goodness . . ." As she talked her English accent became more pronounced, and she picked things up faster and faster. Then she stopped and stared at me, slumped into the chair again, and began to cry once more.

I think, then and there, I grew up a little. Instead of running away again, I sat down on the other chair. "Would you like to talk about it?" I asked.

She raised her head. "Please . . . please . . . you must think me most awfully silly. Really, I don't know what came over me. Really I don't. Is the storm awfully bad?"

I nodded. "Worst I've ever seen. You can't possibly go out in it."

"It was awful of me to come here. I didn't mean to. Not really. I just got on old Nellie's back and rode. At first I didn't even notice the storm."

I kept quiet.

For the first time she looked directly at me. "Did you ever feel you had to go somewhere . . . anywhere away from where you were? No matter what, you had to go? I felt that way this morning when I finally faced the fact that I was . . . oh my God!" She buried her face in her hands again and sobbed. I didn't touch her this time.

She raised her head again, dried her face with nervous fingers, and tried to straighten her hair. "Oh dear, this is so awful. Me sitting here talking like this to a stranger." Then she became wild-eyed again. "Sometimes I feel that if I don't talk to somebody I'll kill myself. These horrid winters are so long . . . so long. Cooped up with the children. Same noses to wipe, same diapers to change, same questions, crying, fighting. And Bert." She stared at me wide-eyed. "Do you think it's possible to hate a man . . . detest him . . . want to kill him, just because he says, 'Well, we've never died a winter yet'? Says it over and over again, every time he comes into the house. Never anything different. Just the same thing."

She looked so pathetically earnest that I burst out laughing. She smiled then.

"No, I don't think it's crazy. I have an aunt who always says, 'The devil finds work for idle hands'. I've lain awake nights thinking of ways to kill her."

"Have you? Really?" She smiled thinly. "I get so I wait for Bert to say it. And when he comes in from the barn in the evening with the pails of milk, do you know what he says? 'Here's the cow juice ready for the whirligig.' And he always does and sometimes I want to scream. Oh God, I get so lonely!" It was a cry of despair.

"Where did you live before you came here?" I asked.

She looked at me. "London. Your name. It's English. Are you from England?"

"No. I've never been out of Saskatchewan in my life. Born here."

"Never? Never in your whole life been away from here? My goodness. How can you stand it? Oh! I didn't mean that. Not really. It's a nice country. It really is. In the spring sometimes . . . sometimes . . ." She was close to tears again, and I suddenly realized that she had never talked like this to anyone before.

"Tell me about London."

"Oh it's wonderful. Really it is. We lived in Lambeth. Daddy was a greengrocer. Had his own little shop. And we had a little house. Not much room, of course. You won't believe it, but there was a big oak tree right in our back garden. You know . . ."

"I've never seen an oak tree. Pictures. And stories. But I've never actually seen one."

"Oh it was lovely. So big, and then we had lilacs and roses – oh, such loads of flowers! Daddy had a green thumb. That's what Mums always said. 'Harold Wilkins, you've got a green thumb.' I loved it. And I had a big dog, Trixie . . . such a nice dog. We have no dog here. Bert says they eat too much. And I suppose they do." Again the far-away look. "I've always loved animals. We didn't get out in the country much, but on the kitchen wall we had a calendar . . . you know . . . one of those picture things. And it was a farm scene. A brook . . . with ducks swimming in it . . . and a swan . . . and the most enormous trees hanging low over the water. And a cow drinking from the brook, and a young girl standing with a switch in her hand waiting for the cow. I always thought I was that girl.

"And, do you know, that picture is what I thought of when Bert said he had a farm. Don't you see, it was the only farm I'd seen. And I thought how nice it would be to live there with the stream, and the grassy banks and the ducks. I can still see that picture when I close my eyes." She closed them and was gone from me again.

"Did Bert tell you his farm was like that?"

"No, no. Of course not. He told me he had a grand farm. A half section. And he gave me such a frightful rush. I was pretty then . . . when I was eighteen." She smiled. She was still pretty.

"He was handsome in his uniform. He really was. And he was so funny. I even thought it was funny when he said,

'We've never died a winter yet.' Oh, and he was so brave going to fight the Hun. A girl would do anything for a boy who was fighting the Hun. So we were married. Mums cried so hard. Daddy scolded her, and I said I'd be back to visit soon. But I never have been. I never have been." She wiped her eyes again with her fingers. "Oh dear, I must be boring you so much."

"Boring me? Lord, no."

"It was so different at home. Always something doing. We would go to the flicks and the music hall every week. And there were my brothers and sisters and aunts. Lord we had so many aunts and uncles, and they were always coming. And then we came here. It was so different."

"When did you come here?"

"In nineteen nineteen. Good God! That's fourteen years ago. I was nineteen years old then – I'm just as old as the century – thirty-three. Bert came home first, do you see. He had to come with his unit. And then I came with my things. I had such pretty things. A hand-done tablecloth that my aunt made . . . Oh dear. And you won't believe it, but a grandfather clock that Uncle Herb had given me. When I got off the boat at Halifax there was Bert waiting for me. And he looked so different. It was the first time I'd seen him out of uniform. Oh dear I was that sick on the boat. I was pregnant, of course." She sighed heavily. "And it seems to me I've been pregnant ever since. And now I am again. I know it. And what will we do with another mouth to feed? Oh my God! We can't look after the ones we've got now. All over again. To go through it all over again." She got up from the chair and began to pace the tiny room.

I had to do something. "Would you like a cup of tea?" I asked. "I could make one in a minute."

She stopped. "I would love that. But please let me make it for you."

I showed her where the tea things were and she made it.

The best cup of tea I'd had in Willowgreen School. With the blizzard raging outside, we sat like any couple and sipped our tea. And as we did so, Mrs. Field became more calm, but I became more bothered. She was becoming more attractive by the minute.

Most accounts of men living alone, it seems to me, omit the most important consideration – the need for a female. Kinsey has established the fact that sex drives are strongest just before the age of twenty, but nobody who has lived alone needs Kinsey to tell him that.

I remember that the physical training and hygiene teacher I'd had in high school – the one who so much enjoyed slapping youths on the bare thighs with his big hard hand – advised plenty of handball, boxing, and hockey as a means of sublimating these biological drives, but my opportunities for those were as limited as for the "normal outlets." And now, to compound my problem, here I was stranded with an attractive woman. But she was married, and to a member of the school district.

At least I could provide her with what *she* needed most – a sympathetic ear.

When she'd washed up the tea things and my breakfast dishes along with them, she told me about that trip from Halifax to the wind-swept desolation of her present home.

"Everything was so strange. Even the trains. And the country so big! From the train window I could see such beautiful scenes: lakes and rivers and rocks and some little farms. And when I asked Bert if our place was like those he'd laugh and say, 'Hell, in Saskatchewan we don't even call that a farm. Wait till you see it, honey. Just wait.' Lord, I was that green. I even asked him about the Indians, and he laughed and said, 'Oh sure, it's just like in the movies. Indians all over the place.' Bert's always been such a one to tease." Her eyes clouded in thought. "I wonder why he teased me so much. I really think that's what started the trouble. That silly talk about Indians, and what happened later."

She shook her head remembering. A shudder shook her frail body. "Then at Winnipeg we came to the prairies, and they seemed so flat. And then the long, long trip to Moose Jaw." She giggled like a little girl. "Moose Jaw. I remember I thought it such a silly name. We changed trains there, you see. And I still had that silly big clock Uncle Herb had given me. I can still see the men taking it from one train and putting it into another. And my trunks with all my things. Oh dear. Then when we got to our station here it was worse. The Millers met us with a democrat. They almost fainted when they saw how much I'd brought.

" 'Here's the girl from London,' Bert said. 'She could only bring half of it. The rest will be along on the next train.' Oh dear, they made such fun of me. Of course there was just room for the four of us and a couple of suitcases in the democrat. The rest had to be fetched later. And Bert hated giving up the time. You see, it was August, getting close to harvest, and he was terribly busy. What a wretched trip home it was. Them pointing things out to me all along the way – gophers, and hawks in the sky, and the ripening grain. They all loved it so much I could see. But it was so strange to me . . . so strange.

"And then there was that horrible first night at home." She shuddered again.

I didn't ask any questions.

"The farm. When I saw it, I could have cried. No brook. No tree. Not anywhere in sight. And the house with no paint . . . and the tiny little barn. And all around just the prairie. I felt so terrible, and I had this nausea from being pregnant. The Millers stayed for supper, of course, and I still don't know how I managed, being so sick and all. And they finally went home, and Bert and I took the lamp up to our bedroom. And then . . . then such a horrid yelling and hooting and banging began outside below our window. You never heard such a racket. And of course the first thought that came into my head was Indians! My God, I thought they'd come to scalp us. I screamed, and, before Bert could stop me – you won't believe this – I crawled under the bed and hid. Well, of course it was just a chivaree."

"A what?"

"Don't you know about chivarees? It's a custom here when a person gets married. All the neighbours, especially the wild ones, come and make a big noise under the window at night, and then you've got to have them in and give them some money or a drink or something like that. Bert was laughing so hard . . . and he dragged me out from under the bed. He had to. I tell you I've never been so frightened in my life. And then he told the others and they all had a good laugh. In fact, they still laugh at it. If anyone says the word chivaree they all look at me and laugh. I am that queer English girl who crawled under the bed. It's bad enough to be English here, but to be English and hide under a bed! They'll never forget. Bert's told the children, and I suppose they'll tell their children, how Grandma crawled under the bed to hide from the Indians that weren't there."

The wild look had come into her eyes again and I tried to divert her. "That first year. Was it very hard?"

"The work was hard. It was harvest time, you see, and for harvest and threshing we had a big gang of men. Some from the East and some, even, from England. At least there was someone to talk to . . . when I had the energy to talk. And then suddenly the threshing was over, everyone had gone and winter had come. God, that first winter. Bert was away often, hauling grain to the elevator, cutting wood on the river bank. Sometimes for a week at a time, and I would have to keep up the fires, carry water, gather eggs, milk the cows, and feed the stock alone." She began to cry, softly. "I was only nineteen, and I'd never done any of those things. My picture of the cow and the swans, where was it? Those long, long nights alone or when Bert was there. It was almost worse when Bert was there." She looked at me and said simply, "He's such a cruel man." Then the sobs broke. "So cruel in every way."

Then she told me a story that even now makes me a little sick to think about.

They kept a few shorthorn cows, which are ideally suited for the prairies because they can be used for milk and meat. During that first fall one of the cows had a calf. It was a hard delivery, and both Alice and Bert sat up with the cow, but it died while giving birth. So Alice took over and raised the calf on a bottle, keeping it behind the stove at first and caring for it as she would for her own child.

"I called it Trixie," she said, "after my little dog at home. Sometimes when I was alone at night that first winter I'd go out to the barn and put my arms around Trixie's neck and just love her. She knew me too, and would come when I called." She smiled at the memory, then shuddered.

One day in February it had turned unusually warm. A soft, dry wind from the southwest licked up much of the snow, and it was like spring. Alice had just taken a batch of bread from the oven when she heard her husband call from the yard.

"Come out here and help me catch that damned calf."

She went out. "What do you want her for?"

"Never mind. Just catch her. Put this rope around her neck and bring her around to the back of the barn."

Glad to get out of the house on such a nice day, Alice pulled on an old sweater and a pair of rubber boots and went out to catch her pet. Through the melting muck of the barnyard she sloshed, laughing and calling out, "Come here, Trixie, you naughty thing. Nobody's going to hurt you." It was a happy, carefree game, but for some reason

Trixie was frightened and hard to catch. Finally Alice cornered the calf, got a rope around her neck, and led her around behind the barn. And, even then, because of her inexperience, she had no inkling of the macabre scene she was about to witness.

Bert was standing beneath a tripod made of poplar poles, the apex of which was about twelve feet from the ground. From a pulley in the apex, a rope hung down to the mud. The other end was attached to the whiffle-tree to which a team of horses was hitched. A neighbour was driving the team.

Before Alice could protest, Bert quickly seized the calf, attached a chain to each hind leg. Then, as it stood there petrified with fear, he took up his twenty-two rifle and shot it between the eyes. The neighbour slapped the horses on the rump with the lines, Trixie swung crazily into the air hind legs first and Bert slit her throat. Then, with one strong stroke, he ripped open her under side from throat to crotch.

"The blood . . . the blood," Alice Field wailed, seeing the sight again. "It poured out all over the snow. And the guts, too. Oh my God, I vomited all over the place and then I ran into the house. I died inside then."

I had never witnessed a butchering myself, but her description of it almost turned my stomach. Nevertheless, I felt constrained to make some defence of this hard-working man. "Uh . . . most farmers have to butcher sometimes," I said.

"I know. I know. But he knew how I felt about Trixie, and still he called me out and never warned me. Afterwards, he teased me about it and told others about me being sick. He likes to kill. Always drowns the kittens as soon as they're born. Poisons gophers. Shoots coyotes. One year he even got a pack of dogs for hunting coyotes."

She stopped and thought it over. Never before had she assessed her husband in so many words. "Perhaps it's just that I don't understand him or this life. It's such a cruel life and maybe a man has to be cruel to survive.

"But he can be kind, too, and thoughtful. When the baby was born – it was due on the tenth of March – he took me to Alsask where there is a doctor."

She told me about that trip then. Two days before what was supposed to be her time, Bert hitched up the team and drove the winding trail of melting snow to Bleke to catch the train to Alsask. They were caught by an unexpected thaw which ruined the road completely, missed the train, and couldn't go further by sleigh. Then her pains began. There was no woman at Bleke, and the situation was desperate. Finally the railway foreman agreed to lend him a handcar and help him get it to Alsask.

"It was one of those kind that two men pump," Mrs. Field explained. "They lifted it onto the track and wrapped me in one of those buffalo robes and we started. The wind got stronger and stronger, and it began to snow. Bert was terribly afraid it would develop into one of these blizzards. And then our luck changed. The wind swung around behind us and blew us almost all the way to Alsask. We made it, but just in time." She shuddered. "I still wake up at night thinking of that ride down the track. It really was awful."

She was shivering again now and began to talk incoherently about her children. I realized that I should get her off the subject. But how? Then I had an idea. Perhaps I could lend her a book. I went into the bedroom and looked through my store. They were mostly plays since I had got into the habit of reading plays during my final year at high school. My eye fell on a thin copy of Noel Coward's most sophisticated comedy, *Private Lives*, which had been produced with great success in London. At least it depicted a different life from that in Willowgreen School. It might take her mind off her troubles.

So I brought it out and suggested that she might like

to read it. She responded as a starving man to a steak. "I used to do dramatics at home, you know. The rector said I was quite good." Lovingly she opened the book and began to read. Then a laugh, merry, young, and spontaneous, burst from her lips. The transformation was miraculous. The drudge had become an animated human being with flushed cheeks and eyes that were alive.

"Could we . . . could we . . . read it together, do you think?" she asked.

At Nutana Collegiate I'd considered myself a hotshot in the dramatic club. This was right up my street.

So we read *Private Lives,* she doing the two female roles and I the two male roles. The afternoon sped by, snow, wind, cold, the bleak, unfriendly prairie forgotten. We were two brilliant, witty people on the London stage. Her laughter brightened those dingy rooms. In the first act scene where Elyot kisses Amanda "violently" she leaned over and lightly brushed my cheek with her lips. As the play progressed, she became more and more intense, and when we were finished, she was exhausted.

"That was so much fun. Imagine living like that . . . away from all this! Why, this isn't living at all!"

To that I said, "Amen!"

It was supper time then, and in the same gay spirit, she prepared our meal. I don't know what she did with Mrs. Montgomery's "canned pork", but it was delicious. The potatoes were creamy and soft. She made a Yorkshire pudding and stewed some prunes. She even managed a table cloth of one of the unused flour sacks that served me as tea towels.

It was the best meal I ever ate in Willowgreen School; in fact, the only decent meal. Alone I never actually laid the table and sat down, but rather wandered about chewing on this or that and swilling tea.

Now, we sat down like two civilized people. "I feel like a regular toff at the Ritz," she said.

We even poured tea into tumblers and pretended it was wine. And for a short while we were carefree and gay, the way young people are supposed to be.

After the dishes were washed we sat on the kitchen chairs with the coal-oil lamp throwing shadows on the wall, and discussed art and literature. Neither of us knew much, but we shared what we did know.

We kept the talk animated but something was happening, something that had to be faced. The storm hadn't let up with darkness and there was no possibility of her leaving. She would be in my place all night. I rehearsed the sentence several times, then finally blurted out that she must have my bed.

"But where will you sleep?"

"I'm not sleepy. I'll sit up and read. I can sleep all day tomorrow. It's Saturday. You need to rest . . . badly."

"I am tired. Thanks awfully. You're most kind."

I felt that she was looking at me expectantly, but I didn't look at her.

She lit my other lamp and went into the bedroom. I got down the book that Harris Montgomery had left me and tried to read, but somehow my mind right then wasn't searching for *A Guide Through World Chaos.*

I wanted this woman, needed her so desperately that my whole body ached. And I knew how she felt. A dozen unconscious little gestures – a hand laid fleetingly on my arm, a turn of the head – clearly indicated an attraction strong enough for the present circumstances. She was a warm, sensitive human being. There was a better than even chance that in that old bed we could enjoy each other immensely.

But something else was eating me. The effect of my strict Methodist upbringing, perhaps, or innate shyness, or uncertainty, or just plain cowardice. Or it may have been my stubborn sense of courtly love – a feeling that sex is a lot more than two people hopping into bed together because the opportunity is there. And, to be fair with myself, I may have had a strong feeling against further complicating her already complicated existence.

I could hear her moving softly in the bedroom, gently stripping the coverings from that white body. Then a pause. I knew she was standing at the door, waiting, wondcring. My mouth went dry as a furnace, my heart beats thundered. If she had opened the door I know I'd have rushed to her and buried all my loneliness, frustration, and anger in the soft folds of her. But I didn't wait for her to open the door. I got the hell out of there as fast as I could.

Up the stairs to the schoolroom I shot, and began pacing back and forth beside the windows. All night long I paced while the storm within me and the storm on the plains blew themselves out. As daylight spread a grey light over the bleak countryside, I noted groggily that a new six-foot drift had built up around the barn door. Another completely hid the front fence. The sky was clear. A flock of snowbirds swerved and dipped over the barn and out across the field. It was a new day to face, with its new problems.

The thought filtered through my fatigue that I was in an extremely compromising position. Regardless of what had happened during the night, the fact remained that Alice Field had stayed in the schoolhouse . . . all night . . . alone . . . with the teacher. This was the fact that would become public information in the district. Would spread by telephone, whispered comment, and innuendo across the land. That queer Mrs. Field stayed all night with the teacher! You know, the one who was so silly about Indians.

The clang of the stove lid downstairs told me she was up. When I went through the door she was standing at the table slicing bacon. She look refreshed.

I asked her if she'd slept well.

"Oh yes, thanks ever so much. But you look terrible. Didn't you sleep at all?"

"Off and on. Look . . . uh . . . Mrs. Field . . . the storm has stopped and . . ."

"Has it? Oh, good heavens! I'd better be going."

"Will you be all right?"

"Yes. Yes. I think I will now. Could you lend me that book, do you think? The one we were reading from last night?"

"Of course. And I have a book of plays by Eugene O'Neill. I think you'd like them, too."

"Oh yes, I would. Ever so much."

"I'll send it home with Bill." Every word was establishing our proper formal relationship.

She started to put on her outdoor things, but I couldn't let her go just like that. "Look," I stammered, "stay for breakfast. You can't go out without something to eat. Please stay."

She hung up her coat again. "All right. Where's the harm." Then she added simply. "Thanks for last night."

To this day I don't know whether or not she meant it as a compliment.

We were finishing breakfast when we heard the sound of sleighbells outside. I looked at Alice Field, afraid that again I'd see that haunted, frightened look. But it wasn't there.

Then heavy footsteps on the floor above. I opened the door and in the dim light saw the mackinaw-clad figure of Bert Field bending his head to miss the landing as he made the turn on the stairs. He outweighed me by twenty pounds and was, I knew, strong as a horse. If he decided to beat me up, there was nobody to stop him.

He came in the door and saw his wife. "Oh, there you are," was all he said.

She looked at him levelly, said nothing.

"Get your things on," he grunted, then turned to me. "How long has she been here?"

"Since yesterday. She was lost. There was no way to . . ." I began defensively, and then realized there was no need for defence. He wasn't mad or indignant or betrayed, just shamefaced.

"She does these crazy things," he said, as a man explaining the behaviour of an unreliable horse or backward child. "Damned if I know why she does them. Course she's in the family way. Maybe that accounts for it."

I glanced sideways at Alice. Her sensitive face was suffused with shame and embarrassment.

"Sorry if she bothered you," Field went on. "I'll take her home now."

I couldn't let her go home like that. Not without some attempt to make him understand her need. "Wait!" I turned to Alice. "Would you mind . . . uh . . . waiting upstairs in the schoolroom? I want to talk to your husband."

She looked at me helplessly and slid out the door. Field turned to me, his expression no longer friendly. "Well?"

"I . . . uh . . . well it's just that she's so . . . uh . . . you know . . . I mean, after her life in London . . . being away from it all . . . her family. It's so damned lonely out here, Bert, don't you see?"

He laid a heavy mittened hand on my arm. His eyes went hard. "Look here, Teacher. You take care of the kids, eh? I'll take care of the woman. And if you mention to anybody she was here, I'll break your back!"

"What? Do you think I would? My God, man . . ."

But he was gone up the stairs.

God damn his paltry, dirt-encrusted soul!

11 Tic tac toe, hockey, and sex

A great deal can be learned by observing children in their off-work hours, but sometimes it's best not to observe them too carefully. This was another useful lesson I learned at Willowgreen School.

The morning and afternoon classes were each broken by a recess period, ostensibly of fifteen minutes' duration but actually varying in length according to the weather, the number of children at school and the extent to which they could involve me in their games. Add to this the hour allowed for lunch – and any kid anxious to get at something else can bolt his food in three minutes – and you have an hour and a half to two hours' free time each day.

When it was impossible to go outdoors, the students, according to their bent, drew pictures on the blackboard, stood in groups giggling, played endless games of noughts and crosses on the board or played a game they had invented themselves and called tic tac toe.

I have a vivid picture of Pearlie Sinclair standing at the front blackboard playing this game with Summer Littlewood. What a contrast! The spindly, dirty, stringy-haired seven-year-old and the rosy-cheeked, neatly dressed, picture-book-pretty nine-year-old.

They drew a big circle on the board and filled it at random with the numbers from one to ten. Then one child closed her eyes tight, was turned around twice by the other and, facing the circle, moved her hand about reciting, "Tic tac toe, around I go, and when I stop I land on this." Then she would score whatever number the chalk landed on. It was strictly an honour system thing with no way of checking on cheating. So Pearlie cheated constantly. Her scabby little hand holding the chalk would go past a big number, the eyelids would flick open, and back the hand would go. Then Summer would laughingly write down the score and take her own turn, eyes closed tight.

I'd watch them fascinated, never quite sure whether Summer knew she was being bamboozled or not. But, of course, she must have known. And to me, this nine-year-old's understanding for a lesser person's ways has always been indicative of something, but I'm not sure what.

When the weather was fit, which meant anything warmer than ten below zero, all the kids went outside to play. I usually went with them, and this provided an opportunity to gauge the effect of my teaching of formal grammar on their everyday speech. It was nil.

After a half hour spent on the proper use of "saw" and "seen" the first thing I'd hear outside would be . . . "Hey Bill. On the way to school we seen two jack rabbits."

A query regarding score would invariably be, "How many goals youse guys got?"

I found this very baffling, until I was talking to a mother, and she told me that, "Heather done real good last term." And gradually I came to realize that in the contest between home and school for the child's speech habits, the school was a sure loser. Seldom was I ever able to counteract the influence of the home. If the parents said "I seen" and "I done" the kids would say it, too, and that was that.

When there was ice, of course, hockey was the game they played. And, early in January, the tag end of a chinook wind hit southwestern Saskatchewan and melted most of the snow. The water ran down to a low spot in the corner of the school yard and sat there on the frozen ground making a rink about forty feet long. After that, every free minute they could find, the children spent on that ice. At recess they played hockey on foot; during lunch hour they put on their skates. And they always conned me into going out with them.

In place of the regulation hard rubber puck with which the game is properly played, they used an end sawed from a poplar pole or a frozen horse turd. There were always plenty of them around. For shin pads – and you can't play hockey without them – they tied old scribblers to their legs. The hockey sticks were the regular kind, usually obtained at Christmas, and tenderly cared for.

Every kid in the school, regardless of age, sex, colour or creed, was on one of the two teams, considerable care being taken to ensure that the teams were of even strength. And every kid played the game as hard and as roughly as he possibly could.

Hockey, it has always seemed to me, is the true expression of the Canadian character. It is fast, rough, audacious, and individualistic. Each year when some second-rate Canadian team finds its way to the winter Olympics or the world hockey tournament, there is a great outcry from other countries about how rough and uncouth and dirty our players are.

Of course. That's the way the game is played. Ice hockey grew straight out of Canadian geography and Canadian temperament. It's an expression of the constant fight against mean climate and conditions. And it's no accident that the best hockey players in the world – and I don't mean those fancy dans from other countries who play international rules, but the pros like Howe, Bentley, and Lindsay – come from the parts of Canada where life is hardest: the mining towns of the Canadian Shield and the wheat farms of the prairies.

Things considered bad sportsmanship in most other games happen as a matter of course in hockey. Nobody gets out of anybody else's way. If a man tries to go between you and the boards, you bang him into the boards. If he tries to go around you, you knock him down. If he eludes you, you take a swipe at him with your stick. That's what it's for. In no other game will you see a player propel a missile as hard as a hockey puck directly at another's head. Few who play this game seriously ever reach the age of twenty with front teeth intact.

Fights on the ice are part of the game. For each player is fighting for his existence. Most serious hockey players are on their way up to professional ranks or have already got there. They know that in this highly competitive game you've got to be the best. And being the best can lift you out of a drab, arduous existence, slogging at the four thousand foot level of a hardrock mine or on a dust-swept wheat field, and put you into a plush apartment in Chicago or New York. Hockey is what boxing used to be to the poor boys of America. The one possible way that those without family prestige, schooling, or money can, as the sportswriters say, make it big. Practically no hockey players are recruited from the colleges of the land.

At its best hockey is the fastest, the most thrilling, the most furiously competitive sport in the world. And if anyone wants to know what Canadians are really like, let him go and watch a professional hockey game in New York, Los Angeles, London, Stockholm – anywhere. For all but a handful of the professional hockey players in the world are Canadians.

Well, having played hockey in Saskatoon school and Sunday school leagues almost since I could walk, I naturally went down to the frozen slough, put on my skates and joined in the game. But not for long. After a few stiff body checks had brought the seat of my pants in contact with the ice, and a few sharp raps on the shin had brought the tears to my eyes, I quit playing and became a referee. Not because I couldn't take it, but because I couldn't hit back. And if you can't hit back in hockey you're dead. There are too many ways of settling scores – real or imaginary – in hockey to make for good teacher-student relations.

I can still see, as vividly as if I were there now, Bob Sanderson taking a stick across the mouth and furiously spitting froth and blood and teeth out onto the ice. He wanted to go right on playing, but I made him come up to the school where I stuffed his mouth full of absorbent cotton to stop the bleeding. Next day he was back on the ice, going as fiercely as ever.

During the late spring it was baseball. When everybody was present and I played with them, we had just enough for two teams. Nowhere else but in a rural school will you find eight-year-old girls, sixteen-year-old boys and a teacher playing baseball on equal terms. And playing it seriously. When the little girls were up to bat the pitcher just automatically moved in half way and tossed soft ones. But those runs counted the same as the others. The baseball games in Willowgreen School were for keeps.

But it was during the in-between season that I ran into trouble. The early spring when the ice was too soft for hockey and the ground too mucky for baseball.

The season when hormones are rioting in all living things. When grass is shooting and crocuses budding. When frogs sing their love songs from the sloughs, roosters chase hens, heifers kick up their heels and coyote couples behave shamelessly. The smell of steaming life is heavy in the air. Big fat bluebottles come out of cracks and buzz on window panes. When boys pull girls' hair and girls shove boys and neither knows why. It's mighty hard then to keep young minds on Troubles in the Roman Senate or Tom Tinker and his dog.

One recess the children poured out of the schoolroom and disappeared completely. Feeling some of the restlessness myself, I went out into the yard to walk around and feel the sun. And then I discovered a peculiar situation. All the children below Grade Seven were playing marbles or tag or squishing through puddles. But of students from Grade Seven up, there was not a trace.

I sauntered over to where Summer Littlewood was pointing out new shoots of green grass to Pearlie Sinclair. "Where are all the others?" I asked.

Summer looked up at me with her innocent blue eyes and said without a blush or a stammer, "In the barn."

My God! In the barn with the door closed tight. What were they doing?

And thus my problem. Each recess, as soon as the bell sounded, boys and girls headed for the barn and banged the door shut. And when they returned there was much smirking and giggling and tossing of heads. Particularly was this true of Violet Sinclair who, like the birds and the bees, was bursting with life.

What could I do? Ask them what was going on? Hardly. Break in on them unexpectedly? Never. But surely it was up to me to do something. Their moral development was at least partly in my care. Some of the girls were old enough to become pregnant and some of the boys were most certainly old enough to make them that way. This was a problem about which the Saskatoon Normal School had been singularly close-mouthed.

Finally I decided on a bold plan. At the far end of the barn, up under the eaves, was a small window. And, luckily, this was the end of the barn that faced away from the school yard, and since it was close against the fence no one ever went around there.

Good! All I needed was some sort of ladder. Down in the basement I found some boards and after the kids had gone home I got busy and hammered them together into a shape that looked as though it would hold me. Then I sneaked it around behind the barn and laid it on the ground, so that nobody coming that way would notice it.

My plan was working well. The next morning at recess the usual contingent skittered into the barn and banged the door shut. The little children played right into my hands by finding some crocuses in bloom on the other side of the school. I had a clear field.

Quickly I slipped out the school door and then stopped. A look-out! What if they had posted a look-out. We always used to. So, I sauntered down to the far end of the school grounds on a pretense of inspecting the fence, and then worked my way back to the barn on the side away from the door.

Now extreme caution was the order of the day. With infinite care I picked my ladder up and leaned it against the end of the barn. From inside I could hear muted argument and some giggling. My mouth went dry and my stomach cramped as slowly, step by step, I made my way up the ladder. I raised my head to look in the window.

Then, disaster. The step near the top let go, I slipped, my pants caught on a nail, and with a terrible ripping sound I fell to the soft ground.

Very carefully I picked myself up and repeated my inspection of the fence back to where I'd started. Only now it was more difficult as I had to keep the seat of my pants facing away from the school.

Luckily, the small ones were still engrossed on the far side of the school and I made it inside unobserved. I slipped down to my rooms, changed my pants, came back and rang the bell.

That night there was a warm, drying wind from the west and next day the grounds were fit for baseball. The children spent all their time outside then, and I never did discover what they'd been doing in the barn.

12 The hot dust of spring

I yearned for spring as an Eskimo in his igloo or a bear in his cave. To get out of that hole in the ground, breathe warm, sweet air, unpolluted by the stench of feet, sour milk, or decaying vegetables. Stroll over the green fields lush with crocus and dandelion. Feel the hot sun on my face and arms, soak in the vitamin D of the ultra-violet rays. I would live again.

In the schoolbooks poets eulogized spring as a time of whispering breezes, soaring larks, bursting buds, and gentle rains. They were obviously thinking of some place else. On the plains, at least during the dirty thirties, spring was a mess.

A few warm winds in March to raise the hopes, followed by vicious blizzards to dash them. Then in April, warm southwest winds licking up the snow. A day or so of water rushing down the gullies into the sloughs. Then the wind is stronger and drier and everlasting. Day and night it blows. And, before you've forgotten the white blizzards of winter, you are into the black blizzards of spring. Dust storms.

In an earlier chapter I said there was nothing meaner,

crueller, or more relentless than a prairie blizzard. There is, of course. A prairie dust storm. Warm winds blow over the tilled fields turning the soil to powder, then pick up the powder and incorporate it into the atmosphere. Wherever air can go, so goes dust. Under window sills and doors, into milk and water and food and lungs. It clogs the nose, smarts the eyes, grits the teeth, and plugs the ears. It covers the surface of floors, desks, and tables with a grey film, gets between the pages of books, into the furthest corners of desk drawers, and onto the dishes on the shelves. Against driving snow you can bundle up. Against dust there is no defence.

Lyle English had a summer fallow field south and west of the school, and I'll swear that some days half of it blew past our windows. Sometimes, looking out, I couldn't see as far as the barn. Nothing but black clouds of swirling dust.

Dust clogged the ditches along the side of the road and buried the fences. In some places the drifts were half way up the telephone poles. Implements left in the field were half buried in dust.

Farmers made grim jokes about the dust. They talked of sowing their neighbours' fields, which was largely true, because sometimes most of the seeded grain blew away and the field had to be reseeded.

"Only way you can tell if the storm is letting up some," Dave McDougall said, "is to toss a gopher into the air. If he digs a hole up there it's still too rough to go into the field."

Along with the dust came those two other hateful children of the drought – grasshoppers and Russian thistle.

The grasshopper plague which had been building for years was reaching its peak. In the fall each mother grasshopper deposits in the soft earth a waterproof pod containing thirty or more eggs. If the next spring is warm and dry, one pod to the square foot produces more than a million grasshoppers to the acre.

And they were all hungry. What first comes out of the

egg is a black, quarter-inch-long wingless grasshopper nymph, and its arrival is perfectly timed with that of the tender green shoots of wheat just poking their heads hopefully above the surface. As the green stuff grows, so do the grasshoppers. They chew up the wheat at every stage. Winged adults clutch the stalk just below the head, sucking out the juice and toppling the head into the dust. Then away they fly to lay more eggs for the next year's crop. Only cold wet weather at hatching time will kill off the grasshoppers, and the spring of 1933 was neither cold nor wet.

Grasshoppers were everywhere. When you walked across the school yard they jumped ahead of you in thousands. Children running along the paths of the baseball diamond slid long before reaching base. Chickens ate them by the bushel, thus spoiling both eggs and meat. Cars on highways had to wear protective screens over their radiators. Grasshoppers got into the milk pails and into the souls of men.

Russian thistle, the third plague of that plagued spring, was, in its own way, as mean as the other two. The most noxious of all noxious weeds, it thrives on drought, so that when the young wheat plants are struggling to make something of themselves in the arid soil, it shoots up above them. Then, being a spreading plant, it further assures their retardation by hiding them from the sun. The whole field becomes a mat of prickly green stems and leaves that by autumn are big enough to foul binders and threshing machines. Then the big branching plants break off at the base and go tumbling across the summer fallow, scattering billions of spiral-shaped seeds that burrow into the ground for next year's crop.

These round, barrel-sized plants piled up against barbed-wire fences until their sheer weight broke the posts. They clogged corrals and banked the sides of outbuildings. And they doubled field work.

Before he could get into his stubble fields with a disk to

prepare for seeding, the farmer first had to dispose of these dead Russian thistle plants. I watched Lyle English working like a slave to prepare his field. First he raked the thistle into piles with the harrows, because, although dry as tinder, they won't "run burn". Then he'd go from pile to pile and light them and with a pitch fork throw loose ones into the flames. And this at a time when getting his seed into the ground a few days late can mean missing a vital spring rain and perhaps losing the chance of any crop at all.

University of Saskatchewan scientists carried out extensive experiments to determine the food value of Russian thistle in the hope that, since it would grow when little else would, it might make up for the drastic shortage of fodder. Finally they were forced to conclude that an animal used more energy digesting the thistle than it gained in nourishment from it.

I've heard farmers planning other ways to use it, and some of their ideas were mighty ingenious. For instance, after having their face and hair scorched from burning it in the field, they naturally thought of some way to preserve that heat for winter when it was so badly needed. Perhaps they could compress the dry thistle plants into solid blocks that could be burned in heaters. No, that wouldn't work; it would just turn to powder. Housewives tried cooking the young plants and serving them as greens, but they were just as tough on the table as in the field.

In fact, sitting around and trying to figure ways of beating the drought and the meagre prices was a favourite sport of farmers in the thirties. And the champion figurer was none other than my friend Harris Montgomery.

One afternoon after the children had left, he drove up to the school in a contraption I'd never seen before. It looked like the bastard result of a mating between a model T Ford and a farm wagon. The body bore considerable resemblance to an automobile. The inflated tires were there and the windshield. But the steering wheel was gone, and so was the engine. Instead, a wagon tongue with whiffletrees attached had been fastened to the front and the whole thing was pulled by a team of shaggy horses.

"How do you like my new Bennett buggy?" Harris shouted, letting himself out the front door and waving a hand towards it proudly. "Just finished it."

"Your what?"

"Bennett buggy. Named after the Right Honourable Richard Bedford Bennett, our esteemed Prime Minister who sits on his big broad post-erior down there in Ottawa without a thought for suffering humanity."

"You made it out of a car?"

"Precisely. A car is of little use without gasoline to run it. Gasoline is unavailable without cash, and you may have noticed there's a considerable lack of that around here."

"I've noticed."

"Can't even afford skunk oil any more."

He was referring to a petroleum product called distillate, which cost considerably less than gasoline but had a tendency to ruin engines and also stunk up the entire car.

The Bennett buggy, just then coming into use, typified the depression on the plains. The automobile part testified to victories of the pioneers over their environment. Its degradation was proof of what the environment could still do to them. Naming it after the Prime Minister was a cogent protest against a government they felt was letting them down.

The Bennett buggy was later followed by the Anderson cart named after James Thomas Milton Anderson who had the misfortune to be premier of Saskatchewan for the first five years of the depression. The Anderson cart was a two-wheeled affair that could be used in place of a buggy. But there were still plenty of buggies around, and so it never really caught on.

"I'd have thought you'd be busy seeding," I suggested to Harris Montgomery.

"No sirree. What's the use of putting wheat in the ground to be blown away? Even if it does grow, there's no price for it. Too much wheat now, they tell us. Why should I grow more?" He pointed a bony finger at me and fixed me with his beady eyes. "Come and sit down and enjoy the sun. God knows we don't see it that much."

We sat on the school steps in the sun.

"Trouble is," Harris said, "we're stultityped in our thinking. All we can think of is growing wheat. Now I've been reading an article in the *Reader's Digest* that really has the idea."

"Such as what?"

"Raise different crops. Wheat ain't the only thing'll prosper on this godforsaken land."

"What else?"

"Snakes, for one thing."

"Snakes?"

"There you go. No imagination. What would you say if I told you there's an annual market for 500,000 snake skins? Now, there's plenty of big rattlers down on the sand plains by the river. God knows we got plenty of gophers to feed 'em." His eyes shone and his beak nose quivered. "Think of it, man! A snake farm! Get the kids rounding up gophers. Why we could make thousands – millions!"

"Uh . . . I suppose there's a certain amount of risk . . ."

"And rabbits!" he interrupted.

"Rabbits?"

"Country's overrun with them. This article says there's a market for millions of rabbit skins. Millions! If we got only a dime each for them, that's close to a million dollars right there. And that ain't all. There's muskrat and goldfish. Goldfish. Now there'd be a good thing to raise.

Course maybe we ain't got the water for it right now." He looked sad.

I thought of an old school joke. "You might be able to cross the snakes and the rabbits," I suggested.

He looked at me coldly. "Yeah, so they'd shed their skins once a year and save us the trouble of pelting them." His scorn turned to wrath. "That's the trouble with everybody. Just sit here and let everything go to pot without trying to do anything about it. Like that wife of mine. Plenty of time to sweep floors but none to go to a meeting."

He got up and climbed into the Bennett buggy. "Well... sit here and get hungrier and hungrier and hungrier. And when you're hungry enough, maybe you'll do something about it. Giddap!"

He flicked his lines and drove off down the dusty road in his Bennett buggy.

That evening the wind came up again and blew steadily for a solid week. Dust filled the air, Russian thistle piled up higher against fences; we were well on our way to another bad year.

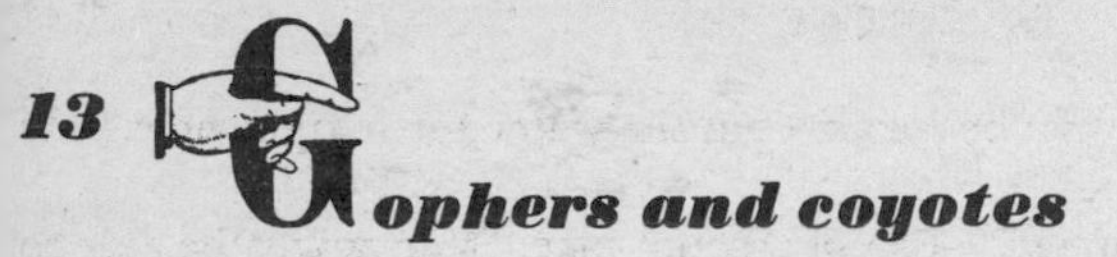

13 Gophers and coyotes

Two other pests entered my life that spring. The first was the gopher. In late March these cute little rascals came up out of their holes for their spring romp, and every kid became a gopher hunter, not for fun alone, but for profit.

I should explain that the common Saskatchewan gopher, the little yellow-brown varmint with the flicker tail, isn't a gopher at all. He's not even a close relative to the mole-like pocket gopher or the renowned prairie dog. No, he's really a ground squirrel – Richardson's ground squirrel to be exact, named after the naturalist-explorer Sir John Richardson in 1820. But he's always been called a gopher, and that's what we'll call him.

This pesky rodent, who then populated the prairie fields at an estimated rate of five or more to the acre, is about ten and a half inches long with a pencil-shaped tail about three inches long. He digs deep burrows in the ground and heads for them at the first sign of trouble; and this is his undoing.

Because of the destructive nature of the beast (each gopher eats about a dollar's worth of wheat a year, and so, on a section of land this amounts to a combined loss of more than three thousand dollars), municipalities usually pay from one to three cents for the destruction of a gopher, proof being possession of the tail. In 1933 the price of gopher tails like that of wheat was rock-bottom low. One cent.

But even this was big money to the farm children of the thirties. A hundred tails meant a dollar, and a dollar cash money was a veritable fortune. Gopher hunting was big business.

The four principal methods of taking gophers were by shooting, trapping, snaring, or drowning out. Since twenty-two shells and steel traps both cost money, the latter two methods were most in vogue.

To snare a gopher you simply chase him down his hole, stretch a binder-twine noose around the opening, and crouch low about twenty feet away. The gopher is by nature extremely curious. Soon you'll hear his wheezy chirp from just inside the hole and his head will appear. Don't move, he'll come further. When he's half way out, yank on the twine and you've got him around the gut.

What you do with him then depends upon how much time you've got and your inclination. Sometimes the children would swing them around their heads and chase the smaller girls with them. Or they'd permit the gopher to run down his hole and drag him back out again. A refinement on this was to swing him around the head and land him in the middle of a slough, if one were handy, and then watch him swim to shore. Gophers are good swimmers.

Drowning out was simpler but more crude and depended, of course, on a supply of water. You simply sprinted back and forth to the slough, fetching water in a leaky can or your felt hat or a bottle. Then you poured it down the hole, until the half-drowned gopher stuck his head through the muddy, weedy mess. Then you clubbed him or let the dog chew him. The trick was to pour the water fast so that you got the greatest benefit from it. Otherwise you heard it gurgling away in the many subterranean passages, and no gopher. And no gopher meant no cent.

Naturally I protested against these practices which seemed unnecessarily cruel, but the children just stared at me as though I were some sort of nut. And, after all, I suppose it was no worse than clipping a pigeon's wings and using him to train purebred retrievers; or ripping the skin off a half-stunned baby seal to make a coat for a lady; or setting dogs to chase a deer until, crazed with fright, it dashes in front of a sportsman's high-powered rifle. And the prairie children at least had the excuse that there was little in their upbringing to refine these natural urges. Besides, they needed the money. Desperately.

Sometimes a shrewd hunter would amputate the tail and let the gopher go, in the hope that he might grow another. As far as I know, this never worked.

As the only representative of officialdom within miles, it was my job to collect the tails and keep track of the score.

So, as the children presented me with these shaggy little wisps of hair, bone and blood, I shoved them into a bottom drawer of the desk against the day when I'd be able to take them to town.

Unfortunately, I forgot all about them.

To tell the truth, with the coming of spring, an even greater restlessness had come upon me. During the long evenings I wandered for miles across the fields toting a beat-up twenty-two rifle borrowed from Harris Montgomery. Now and then I'd take a desultory pot-shot at a gopher. They make perfect targets, scurrying as they do to their holes and sitting bolt upright beside them, chirping and flicking their tails. If you can hit a gopher at a hundred yards, you're a good shot. I never hit one.

Some Saturday mornings I'd start off from school and walk along the trails and over fields, until I came to a farm house. By a happy coincidence this would usually happen around lunch time. I'd hang around watching the men come in from the fields, dust-covered and weary, unhitch their six horse teams, and do their noon chores. Then I'd go into the house with them and sit down to lunch, or dinner, as it was called. It was just as natural for the housewife to put another plate on the table as it was for her to say hello.

If it were a Sunday, the farmer would show me around his place and maybe play a practical joke. All rural folk are great hands at practical jokes, and my farmers were no exception. And once a good one had been got off, it became part of the folklore of the district.

There was the time, for instance, that Sandy Sanderson instructed a greenhorn from the East in the art of harnessing a team of horses, and then gave him a mare and a stud to harness together. The joke came off well; the greenhorn suffered two broken ribs and a mild concussion.

Or the time Wilbur Burke disguised his voice and phoned from Saskatoon to tell the young female teacher that the inspector would be there Monday. And of course all the school kids were in on it and got a great charge out of watching her fuss and fret and get ready for somebody they knew wouldn't be there for months. This one wasn't a complete success, however, because nobody was hurt.

The one of which I was victim came close to being a classic; I almost got killed. I was visiting Leo Ryan, a round-faced Irishman who raised Aberdeen Angus cattle. He took me into the pasture to see some of his choice steers, but one of them turned out to be a bull.

"Gawdamighty!" Leo breathed from behind me. "I didn't know that old brute was loose. Watch out, he's a mean one!"

The bull was about a hundred feet from us. It raised its head, stared in our direction and sniffed the air.

"Will he come after us?" I asked. And I was scared.

"Not if we don't run. Don't let him see you're scared. Keep your eye on him and back slowly towards the fence. Mind . . . don't make any sudden moves. He won't chase you if you don't run."

This was good advice, I'm sure, but somehow the bull

got his wires crossed. For, although I backed away at a snail's pace and kept my eyes fastened on his, he began to come for me – first at a walk, then at a trot.

"What will I do?" I hissed over my shoulder.

"Run like hell!" came the shouted instructions from back at the fence. As soon as Leo had told me about not running he'd beat it for the fence as fast as he could go, which naturally had upset the bull.

I made it to the fence, but with little dignity or aplomb.

The story got a big laugh at dinner and later around the district. To this day I'll wager that any wag can bring down the house simply by screwing up his face and shouting, "Run like hell!"

Some days I kept away from people and walked across the large unsettled tract known locally as "Hudson Bay" (part of the land kept by the Hudson's Bay Company under the agreement of 1870). It was rolling grassland that had never felt the plough and was hence immune from soil drifting. You could walk for hours here, without seeing anything but gophers, hawks, and perhaps the grey shadow of a coyote over a distant knoll. It was here that I had an unforgettable experience – one that did much to make the rest of my stay bearable.

It happened on a day in April. I was walking across the Hudson Bay section when I saw, disappearing over a hill a quarter of a mile away, a figure followed by a small dog. It was just a fleeting glimpse. One moment it was there, the next nothing but the crocus-dotted hillside, the blue sky, and waving grass.

A small shock of excitement ran along my nerves. Could it be the dark lady of the dance? Time and time as I trudged over the empty land I had thought of her and what it would be like to meet her and what I'd say and do. Like most shy boys, I'd always done more thinking about girls than talking to them.

Expecting I knew not what, I hurried towards the

knoll over which the figure had disappeared. When I reached the top of it, I discovered a deep ravine sheltered from the wind. And there, reclining in the grass, reading a tattered magazine, was the figure I'd seen. But it wasn't my dark lady – in fact, no lady at all. It was a tall, swarthy young man of about twenty-five wearing blue jeans, a well-worn windbreaker, and a spotted red handkerchief around his neck.

He looked up when I came over the hill, then dropped his eyes to his book. But I felt this was shyness rather than a desire to be alone. Here was a man to be approached with caution.

I dropped beside him on the grass in the sun. "Hello," I said. "Nice day for this time of year."

His eyes left the tattered magazine (it was of a genre common in those times, known as a "pulp" and I knew it would bear the title of *Ranch Romance* or *Weird Tales* or *Wild West*), looked at me for a second, and then went back to his book. The shaggy little dog that had been sniffing gopher holes and cow flaps sidled up to me and extended a long, sharp nose. I reached my hand towards him but he leaped straight back about four feet.

"I wouldn't try to pat him," the reclining figure said. "He ain't used to people."

"He's an interesting dog. I don't think I've ever seen one like him."

Again the blue eyes flickered towards me and this time remained for a quick inspection. "That's not a dog. That's a ky-yoot."

"A coyote! A tame coyote! Well, imagine that."

"What's so funny about a tame ky-yoot?"

"Well . . . uh . . . nothing really. It's just that I've never seen one up close before. Come to think of it I've never really seen a coyote at all, except in the distance, maybe, and then I couldn't be sure what it was."

"You ain't from around here, then?"

"No." I took a chance. "I teach in the little school about a mile from here."

He sat upright. "A schoolteacher! Well, imagine that. Like you say about the ky-yoot, I've never met up with one of your kind before. Not to talk to. They used to lick me in school and tell me I'd never amount to nothing." He shook his head in wonderment. "A schoolteacher."

I told him my name and extended my hand. He took it and said, "My name's Alec McKay. And my friend here . . . his name is Raffles."

I had met one other man like Alec McKay before, and that was the fall before I graduated from high school, and was pitching bundles on a farm near Nokomis. He was of a breed peculiar to the prairies, an itinerant farm hand, quiet, moderately efficient, and lonely. I remember he'd come along the road carrying a knapsack filled with some cooking gear, a comb, a razor, some odds and ends of clothing, and a dozen pulp magazines. He kept his part of the bunkhouse neat and tidy, and on rainy days, when the rest of us put in our time pitching horseshoes or riding the farm Shetland, he was in the bunkhouse reading.

Alec McKay could have been his brother. I wasn't about to ask him where he came from or was headed. If he felt like it, he'd tell me in his own time; if not, it didn't matter.

"Why do you call the coyote Raffles?" I asked.

"Well, he's sort of tricky and plays a lone hand like the fellow in the story. You know. Raffles in the story."

"Sure, sure. But I've never heard of anyone taming a coyote before. Where did you get him?"

"Oh, I come across him when he was a pup last summer. Farmer I was working for poisoned the mother and father and dug out the pups. Five of them. He clubbed the other four, but I took this one."

"Why?"

The blue eyes half closed. "I don't know. He was kind

of cute . . . tried to chew my finger when I picked him up. Figured he'd make company for me."

He called Raffles over, and the coyote climbed onto his lap and tried to lick his face. Alec fondled the triangular ears. The animal was smaller than I'd imagined a coyote to be, about the size of a shelty collie. The coat was greyish-brown and, because of the spring moult, was coming out in handfuls, giving the little fellow a ragged appearance. The face was pointed with a sharp nose, more like that of a fox than a wolf. The eyes were black and alert.

"Playful little cuss, you know," Alec McKay said, rolling Raffles over on his back and scratching his stomach. The coyote quit squirming and stretched his nose out in sheer enjoyment.

I cautiously put out my hand to stroke his ears. He sniffed it and then extended a pink tongue and licked it. I had a strong urge to become better acquainted with both canine and master.

"If you're not in too big a hurry," I said, "why don't you come over to my place. I can make us a cup of tea and some sandwiches."

"That sounds just fine." He got up and we walked towards the school with Raffles exploring every hole and object along the way. He never missed a thing.

It was the same in the rooms. Like any dog in a new place, he trotted around shoving his long nose into everything – coal scuttle, slop pail, potato sack. The smell of mice intrigued him, and he sniffed behind the cupboard looking for them. I took some scraps from the table and held them up. He reared on his hind legs and snapped them with needle-sharp teeth. Then he lay down at his master's feet, panting like any dog.

I made some tea and sliced cold pork for sandwiches. As we ate, Alec McKay told me about himself. He had been born on a small farm in Manitoba (probably of Métis stock, but he didn't say so) and left home when he was eighteen. "I don't know. Just seemed to have the wanderlust. Figured there was a lot more of the world I wanted to see than that quarter section my folks are starving on."

So he wandered. Working at the harvest here, the spring seeding there. Feeding stock through a winter for a farmer who was wintering in California. Never staying long in one place and always moving west. "I've an idea I want to see them mountains and what's on the other side." The blue eyes went misty. "Maybe I'll get a job on a ship and see what some of the rest of the world looks like."

As he talked he kept looking around my rooms, obviously thinking of something. Finally . . . "You live here all alone?"

"Except for the mice."

"How would you like company?"

The suggestion was so abrupt and unexpected that I instinctively did the wrong thing. "What?" I shouted, and I'm afraid there was a strong note of suspicion in my voice.

"Now just a minute," he said. "It wouldn't be that bad. Nobody bothers you here. You can do pretty much as you like. And it must be terrible lonely."

"It is . . . but . . ."

"You see . . . my trouble is I can't take him with me no more. I want to, but I just can't."

"Him?" Then I realized he'd been talking about the coyote. I began to laugh foolishly.

He studied me "Yeah, I guess it does sound kind of crazy at that. But I don't know what to do. I'm going to work for Stevenson . . . heard he needs a man . . . that's where I'm headed now. And I know he won't want no ky-yoot hanging around. That's why I left the last place. Kept him tied as much as I could, but he howled at night. Oh, I don't think he'd howl if he weren't tied. Besides, it ain't a bad sound. Course I could strangle him and collect the bounty for his ears, but I don't want to do that."

Having recovered from the shock of what I first thought was his proposition, I began to think of the possibility of keeping Raffles. As though he knew his life was in the balance, the small, shaggy animal came over and laid his sharp nose on my knee.

Alec was quick to press this advantage. "Looks like you'll have plenty to feed him."

This was true. I threw out as much food as I ate – stale bread, ripe meat, unused porridge.

Then the clincher. "He'll help keep your mice down, too, and when there's a ky-yoot around there's no danger from rattlesnakes."

He'd hit a tender spot. Actually, I was terrified of snakes, and there were rattlers around. Now that the nights were warm and I kept my basement windows open, I had an almost neurotic fear of a big fat rattler following a mouse through the window and landing with a plump on my bed.

Alec McKay stood up to go. There was pleading in his voice. "Look, Teacher, I can't keep him, and I just haven't the heart to kill him. You take him."

"But what about the school kids?"

"He's used to kids. Fact he's crazy about them. There was three of them in the last place I was. Truth is that's the reason they let me keep Raffles. Those kids liked him so much."

"But what will I do with him when holidays come? I can't take him to the city."

"Turn him loose before you go."

"Why don't you do that?"

"I try, but the old cuss just follows me. I got to get rid of him before I get to Stevenson's. Please."

So, I acquired a coyote named Raffles – from the novel by the same name – and my life was never again the same.

14 Two of a kind

Raffles was my first attempt at keeping a wild animal as a pet, and after my experiences with him and his sad end, definitely my last.

But I embarked on the project with great enthusiasm. Alec McKay had left me a length of chain, and that first night I tied Raffles up in the outer basement. Then, as soon as I got into bed, he began to howl.

The coyote howl has been described as ear-piercing, spine-tingling, haunting. It is none of those things. The coyote is a tenor. He starts off with a few barks, goes into a melodious wail, and, at the end, punctuates the song with a couple of yelps. It is pure melody.

That is, it's pure melody after you get used to it, and when it's not too close. This first night it was very close indeed and fell on unaccustomed ears. So, I got up and let him into my rooms, thinking as I did so that he would be better protection against those rattlesnakes.

To say that a coyote is a restless sleeper is like saying a porcupine has a slightly rough hide. He is no sleeper at all, which is natural enough considering that his habits are nocturnal. As I lay on my back listening, Raffles prowled the room. He rattled pans, nudged chairs, snuffled into bags. Then he was still. Then a loud snap and the crunchy sound of chewing. I leaped from bed and lit the lamp just in time to see a black mouse tail disappearing into Raffles' chomping jaws. It looked as though I'd be exchanging one type of companion for another.

I don't know how many mice Raffles got that first night, but it was close to a dozen. Then, after turning around a million times, he lay down and went to sleep. I dropped off, too, but shortly afterwards was awakened by a distressed whimpering from the coyote. Of course, I realized as a mammal he had natural mammal urges, and unless I did something about them right away disaster would follow.

Here was a dilemma. If I let him out he'd track down Alec. If I didn't . . .

I got up, found the chain, and took Raffles outside. I've always had the greatest scorn for people walking along with poodles on leashes waiting for them to perform. But, after spending an hour on a frigid April night walking a capricious coyote around a school yard, I've become more tolerant about such things.

Finally we were back in the bedroom, and the mouse hunting began again. I can think of a lot more pleasant sounds to lull one to sleep than that of a coyote chewing mice.

The next day Raffles was a complete success. I decided to leave him tied in the basement. But, when the children began to arrive and he heard them talking and rushing about upstairs, he began to howl. So, I fetched him up and introduced him to the pupils. Their reactions varied. The timid ones kept their distance, the affectionate ones wanted to embrace him, and the vicious ones were all for cutting off his ears for the bounty. In any case they were all interested.

When it came time to ring the bell I realized that a coyote lying beside the teacher's desk might make it a little difficult to concentrate on the three R's and so I turned the morning over to nature science.

I hoisted Raffles onto the shiny desk surface where, as is common with canines, he felt very nervous. He slithered around like a Bantu tribesman on skates and, when I grabbed at him with a steadying hand, he mistook my intention and snapped at it.

Thus the first lesson we learned about *canis latrans* is that he has very sharp teeth. When I came up from painting the wound with iodine, I brought one of my bed sheets and we stood Raffles on that. Things went better. We ascertained that he measured 45 inches from tip of tail to tip of nose, stood two feet tall at the shoulder and had a black-tipped bushy tail fourteen inches long. His eyes were slanted like an oriental's, his cheek bones high, the end of his nose snubbed. We also discovered that standing on a sheet on a desk being examined had an adverse effect on his bowel control.

By the time these discoveries had been made, I decreed that we'd learned enough about coyotes for one day, and took him downstairs and tied him up. I was wrong, of course. For the rest of the day we had ample opportunity to learn about his voice.

Gradually the pupils became used to the coyote and he to them. Often he would play tag with them and hide-and-go-seek. He was superior at both games, it being impossible to catch or find him if he didn't want them to. His favourite game, naturally, was drowning out gophers. As an anchor man he was superb, but the children had to be fast to prevent his gobbling up the profitable tail with the rest of the gopher. So, Raffles became a reasonably well-adjusted member of the school.

But not of the district. I soon discovered that, without

exception, the farmers hated him with a deep, steady, vicious intensity. This puzzled me at first, because the coyote is, like the western farmer, a product of a harsh and lonely environment. He and his human neighbours are soul mates – suspicious, lean, hungry, full of natural guile, and furiously independent. The farmers' hatred for the coyote can only be explained as a pure example of the antipathy of like personalities.

Since first coming to the plains, the farmer has waged ceaseless war against the grey ghosts. Traps, strychnine, packs of dogs, high-powered rifles fired from jeeps, snowmobiles, and even aircraft have all been used against him. And all this despite the fact that naturalists and conservationists constantly assure the farmer that the coyote is their best friend. Although he does eat a few domestic fowl and some small stock, the coyote's principal food is mice, gophers, rabbits, birds, and sometimes (although I've never seen this verified) rattlesnakes. But, as the saying goes, give a dog a bad name and he's done for.

The hardy coyote, however, like his human counterpart, refuses to be beaten by his cruel environment. Unlike the wolf, the buffalo, the antelope, the whooping crane, and other persecuted species, he has not only held his own on the plains but has increased in numbers. Sometimes, sitting and talking to Raffles and watching the enigmatic expression on his pointed face, I've thought this Mona Lisa of the animal world has a secret of his own and is waiting for his would-be destroyers to destroy themselves, as he knows they must surely someday do.

And Raffles demonstrated what a short spell of soft living can do for an individual. Since he had plenty of food (he'd eat anything including fruit, vegetables, and cigarette butts), he became sleek and easy going. His long hair grew smooth and soft, and he lost his lean and hungry look. He displayed none of the legendary coyote tricks. Never played dead to catch a prairie chicken or outwitted a gopher. In fact, he sometimes disdained to walk across the room for a bowl of food, lying on his fat belly until it was brought to him. He joined the affluent society.

He followed me everywhere. And although he made my solitary wanderings amusing and meaningful, he was a nuisance on my bi-weekly trips to Lyle English's farm for drinking water. The first time he went with me I forgot all about him until he was in among Mrs. English's chickens. All farmers can interpret the squawking of excited hens and this one definitely spelled "coyote". In two seconds flat Lyle English was out the back door with a loaded shotgun in his hands. It was only by dropping my two pails and dashing forward that I managed to save my pet's life.

"It's all right," I shouted, attaching the chain to Raffles' collar and leading him away.

"What in hell do you mean it's all right? That's a ky-yoot!"

"Yes. A man gave him to me. He's really very intelligent and quite harmless."

"Oh I know all about how smart he is. But as for harmless . . . well, you saw how fast he got among those chickens."

"He won't do it again. I'll put the chain on him before we get here."

"You really figuring to keep that thing?"

"Yes. He's actually like a dog, you know."

Lyle English ran his gnarled hand around the back of his sunburned neck. He'd been in the field since five-thirty in the morning fighting Russian thistle and dust, and he was tired. "You're making a big mistake," he said. "That thing happens to nip one of the kids and there'll be hell to pay. I suppose you know they carry rabies." He turned and went back into the house.

I pumped my two pails full of water and started home. Now, to the similes about the one-armed paper-hanger with the hives and the cat on the hot tin roof, I can add one of my own: busy as a man with two pails of water leading a coyote through a chicken yard.

And believe me I was busy. That streak of grey lightning went around me four times, pinioning my ankles, and then started out. I and the water pails went down onto the manure-soaked yard and I gave forth with some unteacher-like expressions. I tried again, and it happened again. I was just about ready to knock on the door and ask Lyle for the loan of his shotgun, when I got the idea of taking Raffles outside the barnyard, tying him to a fence post, filling my pails at the pump and picking him up on the way past. It worked. But I had an uncomfortable feeling that the English kids had watched the whole performance through the kitchen window.

I couldn't leave Raffles at home alone when I went for water. Locked in the room without me, he chewed everything in sight. Since I owned only one pair of shoes he never did any damage in that line, but he did eat a pair of shorts and demolish a pair of almost-good-enough-to-wear trousers. If I tied him outside, he howled so long and loud that he was sure to attract some trigger-happy farmer. So I took him. And each trip for water became an adventure fraught with suspense, complication, and humour.

Raffles was even more of a nuisance with dogs. The big ones – German shepherds, collies, Airedales – he eluded or befriended (if there are any coydogs, those wild creatures half dog and half coyote, roaming the hills of the Willowgreen district, Raffles is probably the progenitor); the smaller ones he beat up. With a top speed of 45 miles per hour a coyote can outrun anything but a wolfhound. With his sharp teeth and amazing agility he can defeat any dog up to twice his weight. When we entered a farmyard Raffles quickly sized up the situation and made his plans. If I wasn't quick to restrain him, he'd kill a cat, grab a chicken, or attack a dog. This brought all the humans on the run, and I began the invidious task of explaining why I'd brought him there and what I wanted with a fool coyote anyway.

But as time went on I had a much bigger problem: what to do with Raffles at the end of the term. My chances of disposing of him the way I'd got him were slim. Several of the school children would have taken him, but their parents quickly vetoed the project. To these farmers, dogs and cats weren't so much pets as farm hands. If any animal couldn't earn its keep by herding cattle or catching mice, what was the sense of keeping it around the place? And if I turned that lazy, over-confident coyote loose in the district he wouldn't last two days. It was a problem.

But as the roads began to dry up another problem was more immediate. One of these days, as surely as May follows April, I was going to have a visit from the inspector of schools.

15 An inspector calls

To the beginning teacher the school inspector is an ogre. One day when you least expect him, when your brightest pupils are all absent and all the dullards present, when your work is unprepared and your spirits low, without warning he opens the door at the back of the room and is upon you. During my years of teaching on the prairies, I often speculated on how a man in a car could approach an isolated schoolhouse unnoticed by children who spend two-thirds of their time gazing out the window and can spot a jack rabbit at half a mile. Finally, I concluded that, ogre-like, inspectors have supernatural powers.

Certainly the effect of my first inspector verged on the supernatural.

One of the first things I'd asked McDougall was when could I expect the inspector.

"Well," McDougall said. "He never comes in winter. Too far for a town feller to drive in a cutter. But around about the first week in April when the roads are barely open, you'll see his old Essex meandering down the road to the school."

He laughed and spat. "Don't know how many times I've pulled that car out of the mud."

I wished he hadn't told me about seeing that car come meandering. From my position at the front of the class I had a perfect view of that road, and, from the beginning of April on, I never really took my eyes off it.

Besides, I kept a good sample lesson for each grade tucked away in a desk drawer, ready to be produced on the fatal day. And I had lesson plans ready and the register up to date and an elaborate time-table tacked to the wall. Once or twice I even looked at it.

I even cleaned up my rooms, knowing that he'd probably stay for lunch and I'd have to cook for him. So, each morning I swept the floors, washed and put away the dishes, cleaned out the empty milk and pork sealers, and made my bed. And each morning I tied up poor Raffles. It wouldn't do for the inspector to find a coyote lying peacefully beside the teacher's desk.

And I watched that road. Like a jack rabbit watching for a fox, I watched it.

When the snow first melted, the road was one long, slushy mudhole that a buggy could scarcely navigate. And of course this was when I watched it most carefully. The children soon caught on (kids catch on to everything) and began watching it with me. And, to add spice to the game, when I wasn't watching one of them would give a loud gasp as though he'd seen trouble coming. They didn't exactly laugh when I swung around like a scared cat, but they grinned into their books.

The second week the road was dry and my troubles were worse. Now the local farmers were using the road with Bennett buggies and the occasional Model T, indistinguishable at a distance from an Essex. Every cloud of dust sent my heart into my throat and my mind to planning, but it was always a false alarm. But even schoolteachers, like rabbits, must relax their vigil sometime, otherwise coyotes would starve and inspectors would catch nobody; and inevitably I began to think less and less of the fatal day.

Easter came and went – because of the long winter holiday we took only Good Friday off – but the inspector didn't. Gradually I slipped back into my practical, if unorthodox, methods, concentrating on the three R's, giving most of my instruction time to the primary grades and leaning heavily on the encyclopaedia. Down below my rooms degenerated to their slovenly state with ragged yellow cigarette butts adorning the table edges, dirty dishes piling up, papers, books, and clothes cluttering the floor. Physically and pedagogically, I was a mess.

Then, one morning when the lark definitely wasn't on the wing, nor the snail on the thorn and all was wrong with the world, the inspector came. I had slept in, failed to shave, hadn't put on a fresh shirt, and was in a fog. Half way through the morning I had got myself lost in the sideroads of a Grade Ten algebra question and neither Alan nor myself could find our way. The Grade One children were messing around with plasticine, having been neglected for a full hour. Grade Five were making a four-foot-long map of Canada with flour and water and sand and sticks and other messy stuff. The rest of the children were working on encyclopaedia projects. In the midst of all this, as I covered a section of blackboard with x's and y's, I gradually became aware that the scratching of chalk was the only sound in the room. I knew He had arrived.

The strangest damned things plague schoolteachers. For instance, my first terrified thought at that moment concerned the condition of the zipper on the front of my pants.

The fly, I realize, is an indelicate subject, but sometimes to the schoolteacher it transcends all others. I remember once teaching a particularly well-prepared English lesson to a Grade Ten class. I was in good form; words and phrases sprang to my lips like hounds to the chase. I gesticulated, leaped, and roared. But I couldn't seem to hold the class's attention. They looked at each other, at the floor, out the window – anywhere but at me. They didn't snigger, smirk or wink; just seemed embarrassed. Then, as so often happened when baffled, I lost my temper and gave them a severe tongue lashing. At recess they left the room sadly. Then I discovered that my fly was undone – top to bottom. Fortunately, I hasten to add, my shorts were impregnable, but still it was a devastating thing.

And what can you say after an experience like that? You can't very well apologize. "I'm sorry I lost my temper, class, but I didn't know my fly was open." But you have to face them again, teach them another lesson, and of course they'll know that you know they noticed. Oh Lord! You have to be a schoolteacher to appreciate the feeling.

So, on that May morning in Willowgreen, when the silence of the room told me I was about to meet my first inspector, I surreptitiously slid my hand down the front of my trousers, found all secure, took a deep breath and turned around. The man standing at the back of the room was like someone from another world. He wore a well-pressed charcoal grey suit and a white shirt and tie. His shoes were shined, his grey topcoat immaculate, and his bowler hat new. For a moment we stared at each other, the hunter and the hunted, face to face at last.

I started down the aisle towards him, but he waved me back. "Just go ahead with what you're doing. I'll look around." He took off his fine new coat and laid it with his fine new hat on an empty desk. Then he walked along the aisle bending over to see what each child was doing. I turned back to the board to wrestle with the algebra question, but my mind was really on those filthy rooms below and how I was going to keep the inspector out of them.

It could be said, to paraphrase the French proverb, that

when the inspector comes in the door, knowledge and perception fly out the window. With the arrival of Mr. Woods, the children of Willowgreen School were stricken dumb. When I most wanted them to be presentable and brilliant, they could only grin self-consciously, hide their heads, blush, mumble, and forget everything they'd ever learned.

Of course, a lot of this was due to the asinine questions that are traditional with inspectors. At that time most of the Saskatchewan contingent were products of the old Ontario school system, and I've actually heard one ask prairie children to name the counties of the southern part of that province. Under prevailing conditions I considered it lucky if the children knew there was a province of Ontario and had some idea of its location.

This inspector asked the Grade Five class to name the capital of Canada. After some hesitation, Sammy Sinclair's hand went up and he said he thought it was the letter "C". This fetched some grins from the rest of the class, but nothing from Mr. Woods. Then Summer Littlewood salvaged our reputation by saying that it was Ottawa.

"Fine," beamed the inspector. "And where is Ottawa?"

"In Ontario . . . sir."

I was proud of her. But he wasn't through with that. Not by a long shot.

"On what river?" he asked.

"The Ottawa, sir."

My chest expanded with pride. But he still had a clincher.

"And?" He looked at her expectantly and, when her face went blank, shifted his gaze to the other blank faces. "Can anyone tell me what other river runs through the city of Ottawa?"

The grin faded from my face. But, wonder of the age, it turned out that Charlie McDougall's granddad had been a hod carrier at the building of the Rideau Canal and had lived in Bytown (the early name for Ottawa), and he had told his grandson about it. Up went the dirty hand. "The Reedoo River."

I felt like Tunney after the Dempsey victory but my triumph was short lived. "And what other river besides the Rideau enters the Ottawa near the capital?" the inspector asked.

Nobody could answer. The inspector had beaten us again.

And he went on to follow this victory with even more crushing ones. The children quickly figured out that this man was too unreasonable to take seriously and disdained to give reasonable answers to the simplest of questions. The payoff came when he asked Jake Stevenson to describe the mouth of the Clyde (Woods had spent his last holiday touring Scotland) and Jake told him that he figured it was about the same as that of any other horse.

After his match with the children the inspector took on me, an even less formidable opponent. After checking my register and time-table he asked to see my daily journal, explaining in response to my blank look that it was a day-by-day record of the progress of each class.

He had me, of course. With nine grades I was far too busy preparing lessons and teaching them to make notes on it. This led to a lecture on the advantages of orderliness and neatness. With a sideways glance at the children he even added a bit about cleanliness. And it was getting close to noon.

Then, as inspectors will, he began to poke through the drawers of my desk. Like most teachers' desks this one had one long, shallow drawer above the knee hole and four narrower, deeper drawers down the right side. Beginning at the top, Woods opened each drawer in turn, poking around with his finger, pursing his lips, and shaking his head. From the far front corner of the room, where I was conducting a reading lesson, I saw from the corner of my eye that he'd reached the bottom drawer.

Then I remembered.

"No!" I yelled, dropping the reader and racing to the desk.

But it was too late. He'd opened the drawer and there they were – one hundred and fifty-seven festering gopher tails, crawling with maggots. A fetid, reeking mass.

Inspector Woods jerked back so fast he almost upset the swivel chair. I grabbed the drawer and rushed outside with it, followed by the anxious stares of the boys. After all, rotten or not, those tails represented cash.

After that everything was pretty anticlimactic.

I was determined not to invite this man down to my rooms. He just wouldn't understand. I wasn't even sure that he knew I lived in the basement. My usual practice was to slip down and make myself a lunch while the kids bolted theirs in about five minutes and tore outside to the more important business of gopher snaring. But I couldn't do this then without inviting Mr. Woods down for a hot cup of tea. So, I decided on one of those ridiculous moves that are always getting me into trouble. I pretended that it was my practice to skip lunch altogether.

It turned out that Mr. Woods had a thermos of steaming coffee with his lunch, and so, while he sat munching chicken sandwiches and cake and swilling coffee, I sat there hungry as, to borrow a good prairie simile, a she-wolf with a litter of pups and a tapeworm.

The afternoon was much the same as the morning and, when Woods was about to leave, he looked at me slyly and said, "I understand you have a teacherage in the school. I'm curious to see how they've fixed you up."

What could I do? Momentarily I toyed with the idea of refusing this direct request, or even pretending that my door was stuck. But lethargy and confusion had so taken over that even this was impossible. I led the way downstairs. Showed him the furnace and the chemical toilets and even the small heap of coal left over from the winter. Then, finally, I opened the door of my room and he poked his nose inside.

He didn't go in, just stood on the threshold like a society matron viewing a tenement slum. (It wouldn't have been quite so bad if Raffles, unused to being shut up, hadn't chewed up the carton of potatoes and made a mess on the middle of the floor.) Then he turned, went up the steps, got into his nice new coat and hat, shook hands limply, and left.

As I sat alone on the school steps watching the square end of the Essex getting smaller and smaller down the dusty prairie road, I was lonely and sad. Sad to think of what his visit might have been had I not been so numbed by solitude and he so unbendingly official. Of how we might have sat and talked of education and the problems peculiar to these ragged but valuable children. Of how he could have opened their minds with tales of places he had been and they would never be. Given them some concept of the great land they were a part of, but didn't know. Instead, he'd carped on details and I'd acted the bumpkin.

And I realized then and there that my validity as a person required that I leave this place as fish leave a stagnant pool. My mind, as well as my lungs, was filling with dust. I was little better than a hermit whose thoughts were becoming as sparse as his conversation. My very sanity demanded that I get the hell out.

16 The dust clears

Ever since my school teaching days, the month of June has been special. It was the month of exams, when pupils would either progress or stay put. It was the month of heat and growth, for even in those arid days, there was some greenery in June. But, most of all, it was the month of liberation.

No one but a teacher can know what liberation from a schoolroom means. It's not just release from work. If so, there would be some justification in the charge by non-teachers that teachers have it pretty easy ("Six months holidays twice a year," my older brother used to say). No, it's freedom from something much more onerous. From having constantly to be on top of a situation, be policeman, lifeguard, mother, father, mentor, all in one. And the really frightening realization that you're working in vital clay. A bankrupt business man loses only his own or others' money; a bankrupt teacher helps lose a life.

My immediate concern, of course, was preparation for exams. These were sent out by the provincial Department of Education and were marked by the teacher. They arrived in sealed envelopes bearing the explicit instructions that they weren't on any account to be opened until the moment of the exam.

I just about opened them the moment I laid hands on them, reasoning that under these conditions the exams weren't valid anyway, and the end justified the means. But a niggling sense of not wanting to cheat, and the realization that I alone would judge who was to be promoted anyway, made me change my mind. I'd pass the children on the basis of the three R's and that would be that.

But, of course, this wouldn't do for Grades Eight, Nine and Ten. Some of these children might well be going to other high schools if financial conditions improved (they didn't until six years later, when the war provided a need for wheat and people), and they needed some standard on which to be graded. But, since I'd given them more than half of my instruction time and they'd worked hard, I was confident they would make it without any illegal help from me. So, I didn't peek.

I had other decisions to face.

Motivated by the consideration that, although I wasn't great shakes socially and had poor taste in pets, I was at least moral and healthy and on the spot, the board invited me to return for another term.

"We can't pay you any more money," Lyle English explained. "But from what I read in the papers you can't get much more anywhere else. Might as well hang on to what you've got."

"Do you mean," I asked, "that you can't pay any more . . . or just realize that you don't have to?"

"Well, there are plenty of teachers around, I hear."

"Yep. That's a fact."

"And I don't see how you could do much better. After all you've got a place of your own at the school there."

"Right again."

"Well?"

"Nothing doing."

I'd at least brought a look of surprise to his face.

"Door mats are made to be walked on," I continued.

"Now look here. Nobody's got any money. We're all just getting by . . ."

"Oh, I don't blame you. It may be right enough for you to get a teacher as cheaply as you can. It's your school, and they're your kids. But, it's not right for me to be part of it. Unlike you, I'm not bound by these conditions and this place. I can quit."

"Well . . . maybe so . . . but . . ."

"That's one of the things I've learned here, Lyle, and it feels kind of good to know it. I haven't any idea what I'm going to do. But I'm not going to live alone and eat rotten meat and stagnate."

"We might manage to do a little better. The kids all like you. . . ."

"Don't worry about it. I won't stay under any conditions."

And that was that.

Harris Montgomery had other arguments, which he presented during a berry-picking expedition to the river bank.

Berry-picking was an essential part of the farmers' life. Wild strawberries ripened along the sides of the roads and railway tracks. Gooseberries were occasionally found in coulees. Even rose haws were made into jam. But the berry that was an integral part of the diet was the saskatoon.

A good case could be made for the saskatoon berry being the fruit that made life on the prairies possible. The Blackfoot, Gros Ventre and Assiniboine Indians picked them by the skinful, dried them and incorporated them into their pemmican, thus getting their protein, vitamins, and sugar all in one concentrated bite.

As a boy I remember the annual berry-picking expeditions being as important as the potato crop. Everybody went; everybody picked. We came home with washtubs and boilers filled with the plump blue berries, and for the next couple of weeks mother was busy putting them into sealers. It was a bad winter, indeed, that we entered without four or five dozen quart sealers of saskatoon berry preserves in the basement. And we were town people.

And there's no doubt that during the thirties when apples, oranges, and almost every other kind of fruit were scarce as new cars on the prairies, saskatoons saved many from vitamin-deficiency ailments. By spring you were so hungry for something fresh you'd sit for hours in the sun, pulling grass roots and eating the tender ends. And when berry time came you stuffed yourself with all you could hold.

So, I went berry-picking with Harris Montgomery and his assorted relatives. I took Raffles, of course; he trotted beneath the Bennett buggy like any farm dog. When we got there I discovered that part of Harris's philosophy included the idea that while the others picked, he should sit in the sun and talk. It was, in fact, the only part of his thinking with which I could be in complete agreement. So, while the women picked and the children chased each other and had a great time among the trees (the Saskatchewan river bank, about two hundred feet wide and tree-covered, is an oasis on the prairie), we sat and discussed matters of great moment.

"The movement needs young blood," Harris argued.

"It's not getting mine."

"No, no, no, you don't get my meaning. A great new march to freedom is afoot and will shoot like a meteor across the sky. Look at what Roosevelt is doing in the United States."

"Wonderful!" I conceded.

"But he's not going far enough. We've still got poverty in the midst of plenty. The vested interests are strangling the economy. Nothing but out-and-out socialism will save us."

"I'm confused. What is socialism?"

"Why . . . why . . . it's every man according to his need. Production for use instead of profit. State ownership of the means of production."

"But here the means of production are land and machinery. Would you socialize them?"

"Well, maybe not right at first. I'm thinking more of factories . . . you know . . . things owned by the big capitalists."

"And where do I fit into all this?"

"Why, youth. Of course. We need youth. Spirit of the future. Don't you agree things need changing?"

"You're damned right I do."

He leaped to his feet. "Good! Wonderful! We've got to get a strong committee going here. And we need youth. But the wife says you're talking of leaving."

"I am."

"But . . . but . . ."

"That's the change I was thinking of. You're trying to argue me into politics, when I'm pretty sure I have no talent for it. You urge me to join your socialist movement, when I'm not sure I agree with it or even understand it."

"But things are terrible."

"I agree. They were terrible back before 1929, too. You weren't hungry, but millions of people around the world were. People died who shouldn't have. Others, who by every criterion should have been dead, lived and prospered. It's no different. There seems to be little justice in the world. The rich get richer and the poor get poorer. But that's the way it's always been with human beings and I'm damned if I can see how what you're proposing is going to change it."

"You're pretty bitter for a young man."

"Nope. I was when I first came here. Bitter and sorry for myself. But you people educated me out of that. I know that

I can either stay here and go on being bitter or I can leave. I'm going to leave."

He peered out over the wide, muddy Saskatchewan River then. A beak-nosed, stubble-faced reformer, who had an idea and got his words mixed up trying to explain it. "I don't know," he said at last. "Maybe all those things are inveterable, as you say, but I like to think they ain't. And I'm going to keep on trying to prove they ain't. This world's got to be a better place than you see it."

So, that was that.

I noticed then that there was no sign of Raffles and realized I hadn't seen him since we sat down. I called, but he didn't come. And when we loaded the full wash-tubs into the Bennett buggy there was still no sign of him.

We all called, but only the echo of our voices from the far shore and the cry of the curlew answered us. And, because the sun was getting low and we had eight miles to drive, we couldn't wait longer. I never saw him again.

So ended the only real friendship I'd established at Willowgreen School. Perhaps he met a lonely female there on the river bank. I hope he did. Or perhaps in some mystic canine way he knew the problem – God knows I'd told him about it often enough – and took the only logical course. I didn't worry on his account. He'd quickly adapt to the necessities of life and take on the tricks of coyoting. Anyway, I've never forgotten him. He was a worthy representative of a tough, uncomplaining, resourceful, fun-loving prairie breed.

After the berry-picking episode I was too busy marking exams, doctoring the results, and making out report cards to think of much else. On the final day of school I passed out the reports and the children received them impassively. They had all passed into the next grade and most of them deserved it.

Then they sat looking at me and I stood looking back at

them. I felt there should be something wise and useful to say, but nothing came. I dinged the little bell on my desk, and they filed out. I heard them laughing and shouting and comparing report cards. They were in their own child world where no adult can ever find a place. I think they appreciated me as much as the next teacher and at some time in the future might even consider I'd done them some good. As for me, I could at least be confident I'd done them no real harm.

Before he left, Carl English sidled up to the desk and dropped a note. It was from Lyle and it said that, since it would be a lot easier if I caught the main line train at Alsask than the local at Bleke, he'd drive me there in his car. He'd pick me up at six the next morning, the note said. I knew this meant he'd have to take a half day off field work, and I appreciated it.

Down in my rooms the realization that I was free suddenly hit me. I was overtaken with a wild giddiness. I shouted aloud and sang and gave little leaps into the air. I would be with people again. Talk to them, argue with my brothers, fight with my sisters. Hold the hand of a girl. See a movie. Walk on a concrete sidewalk.

Then, I don't know why, I tore into those rooms and cleaned them thoroughly. Swept, scrubbed, scoured everything in sight, even the top of the stove. Then I ate some supper, packed my trunk and wrestled it upstairs, and went to bed for the last time in Willowgreen School.

Sharp at six the next morning Lyle English chugged up to the school in his 1929 Model A Ford. I was ready, having been up at five, cooked my breakfast, washed my dishes, said goodbye to my mice, and left my basement home forever. Never since that time have I really been comfortable in any room below the surface of the ground.

The drive to Alsask was a silent one. The day was bright and, with the contrariness of nature, windless. The fields were green with wheat already in the shot blade. Gophers scurried across the road, and occasionally we'd feel a jar as a wheel went over one.

Something was bothering me. All that I was leaving I'd hated during the past six months – the loneliness, frustration, poverty. But there was an annoying pull backwards, a definite reluctance to leave. Was it the attraction of habit (a released prisoner might miss the cell for a day), or was it something more? Had this place and these happenings become a part of me, affecting to some extent my thoughts and actions for all time?

The Model A bumped its way into Alsask and drew up to the station platform. It was the usual scene. A flat-topped dray, pulled by a team of enormous Percherons, stood ready for loading. A Dodge sedan with the word "Taxi" painted on the side, was next to it. On the platform were a dozen or so full five-gallon cream cans waiting shipment to the city. Two small boys and two girls, recently released from school, ran back and forth over the wide planks. Their mother, who was taking them to the city for a visit to the dentist or for music lessons, stood patiently by.

Off to one side a pretty girl and a farm youth were in urgent conversation. She kept looking up the track for signs of the train; he stared fixedly at her as though the force of his eyes might keep her there.

Lyle English and I got the trunk out of the back seat of the Model A and set it on the platform beside the cream cans. Awkwardly he extended his right hand with the middle finger missing. "Well, Teacher, good luck," he said. "I want to thank you again for what you done for Betty and Carl. They both got along better this term than they have in a long time."

I shook his hand and thanked him again for driving me over.

The train pulled in. The mother got her four children

onto it. The cream cans and my trunk were loaded. The drayman hoisted some cartons and machinery parts onto the dray. The young girl held her swain's hand for a moment, brushed his cheek with a quick kiss, and hurried up the metal steps into the coach. I followed and took the seat beside her. She was even prettier than I'd first noticed. The farm boy came to the window and gazed in with worried eyes. She waved a small hand and turned to me. "Lord, I wish this train would start."

"Me too."

Through the window I could see Lyle English's Model A kicking up dust as it turned into the road back to Willowgreen School. In the six months I'd known him he'd never once called me by name.

THE END